AF283924

TOKYO PRECINCTS
A curated guide to the city's best shops, eateries, bars and other hangouts

￥980
スタ ￥950
ラ ￥980
ソース ￥980

ジュース
）
ー
￥300で
ワイン
（赤・白）

LUNCH
TIME
限定
2人前 ￥500
（一人前 ￥280）

当店オリジナルの
HONEY&ONION
ドレッシングを使った ￥630
FRESHな
サラダです！
ドレッシングのお持ち帰りもどうぞ！

HONEY & ONION
DRESSING

NEW
FR

TOKYO PRECINCTS

A curated guide to the city's best shops, eateries, bars and other hangouts

STEVE WIDE **AND** MICHELLE MACKINTOSH

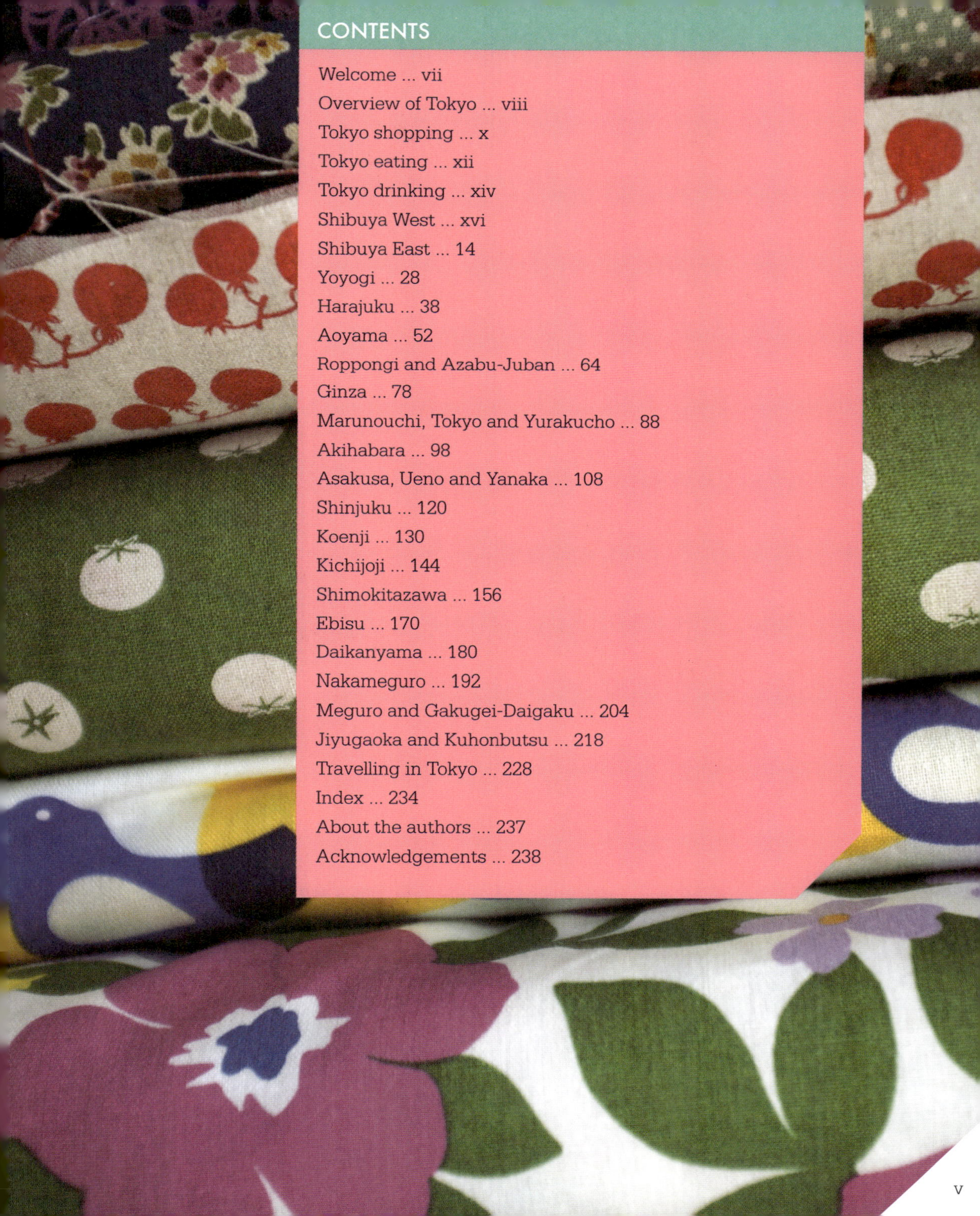

CONTENTS

24
JUN 80T6
ランチョンマット A4 玉かすり オレンジ　40円
ランチョンマット A4 玉かすり カラシ　40円 + 税
40円 + 税
CHICKEN BREAST
LIVER

Konnichiwa and welcome to *Tokyo Precincts*. Tokyo is our favourite city in the world! It's a place of eye-popping fashion, incredible food, cat cafes, hole-in-the-wall bars and train stations as big as city blocks. There are towering buildings with neon signs next to warren-like alleys full of tiny, old-world eateries. The shopping is dangerous! You'll be cramming your bags with toys, the latest gadgets, homewares and beautiful crafts. There is so much to love here, and we hope you'll uncover your own favourite things.

Tokyo is a gigantic city, but it's made up of smaller cities, each with its own unique feel. If you tackle Tokyo one part at a time, you'll get a handle on it in no time. *Tokyo Precincts* is divided into 19 precincts, and for each we've picked our favourite shopping, eating and drinking experiences. This is our personal take on the city, which we hope you can use as a springboard for your own adventures.

You'll most likely use the train system to get around. The trains are fast, always on time and crazy fun, from the cute ads showing on tiny TVs to the sardine-can crunch at rush hour. We've included station exit information for each review and some simple maps to help you get around (it's easy to get lost). You'll also find some (hopefully) handy tips on navigating Tokyo, etiquette, food, drinks and so on (*see* pp. viii–xiv and pp. 228–233), which will help make your trip go as smoothly as possible.

So launch yourself into Tokyo's precincts! Once you get your bearings, there is no end to the fun, amazing shopping and eating, friendly people and unforgettable experiences. There is simply no other place in the world like Tokyo and we hope you love it as much as we do.

Steve Wide and Michelle Mackintosh

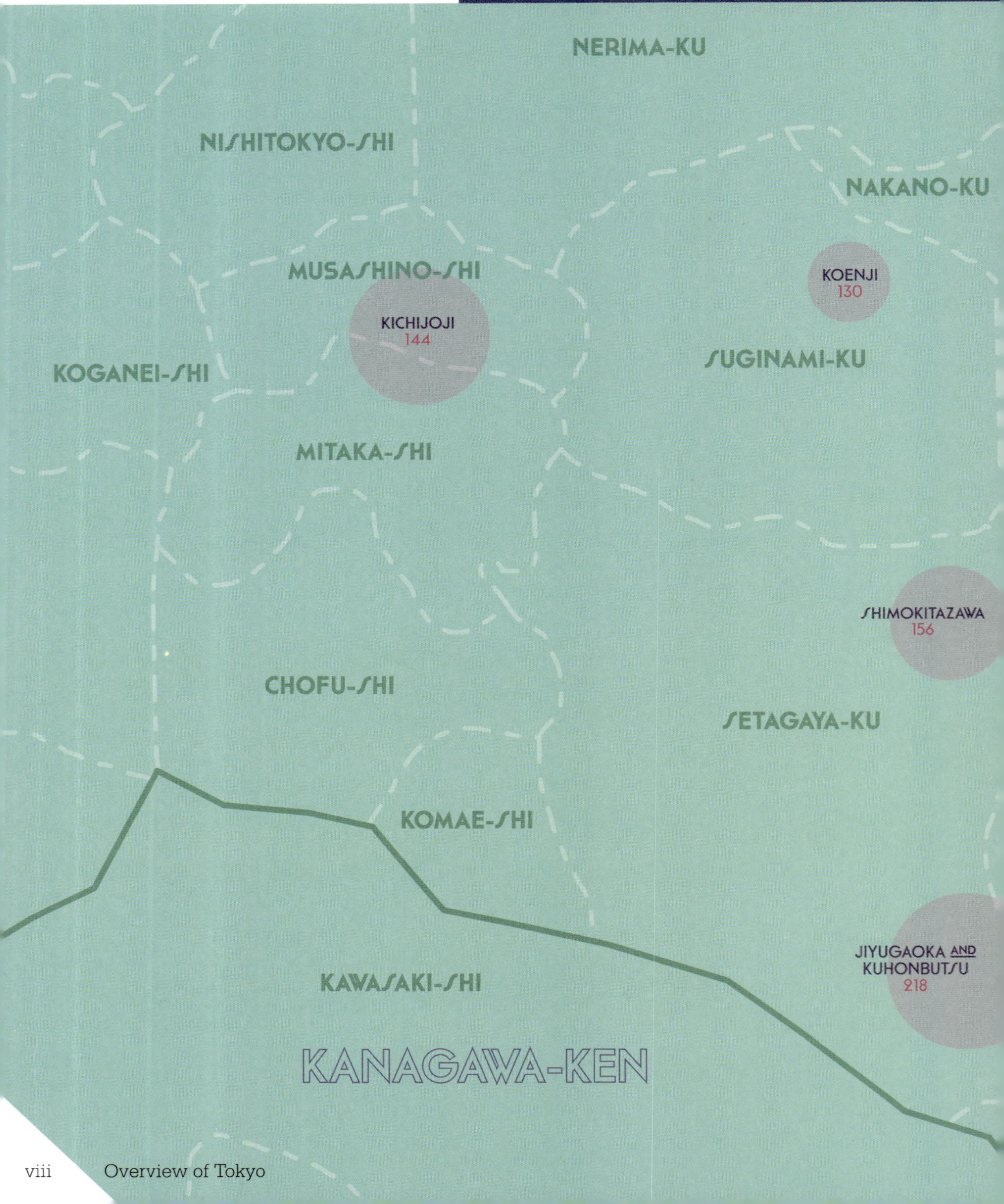

NERIMA-KU
NISHITOKYO-SHI
NAKANO-KU
MUSASHINO-SHI
KOENJI
130
KICHIJOJI
144
SUGINAMI-KU
KOGANEI-SHI
MITAKA-SHI
SHIMOKITAZAWA
156
CHOFU-SHI
SETAGAYA-KU
KOMAE-SHI
JIYUGAOKA AND
KUHONBUTSU
218
KAWASAKI-SHI
KANAGAWA-KEN

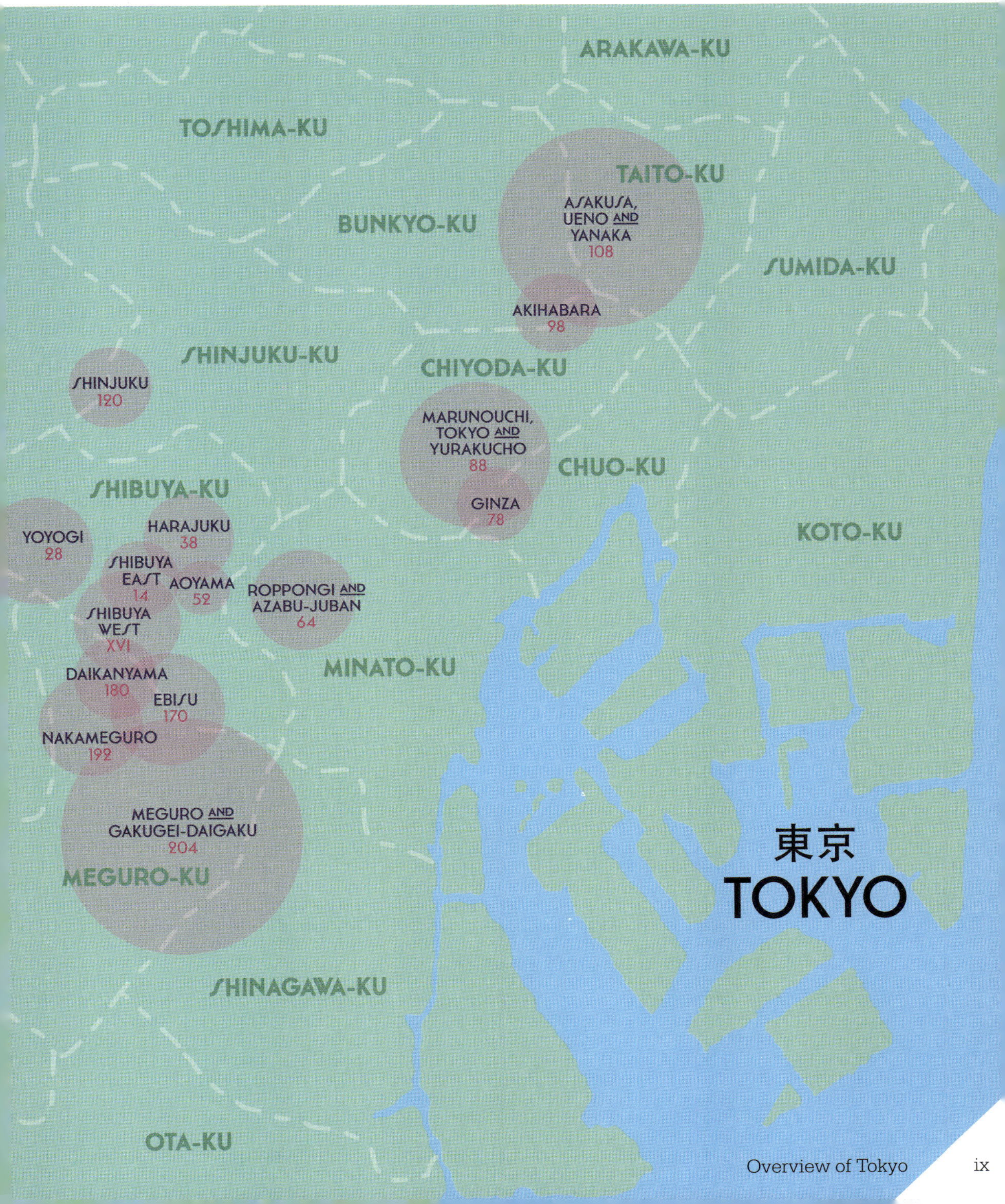

ARAKAWA-KU
TOSHIMA-KU
TAITO-KU
ASAKUSA, UENO AND YANAKA
108
BUNKYO-KU
SUMIDA-KU
AKIHABARA
98
SHINJUKU-KU
CHIYODA-KU
SHINJUKU
120
MARUNOUCHI, TOKYO AND YURAKUCHO
88
CHUO-KU
SHIBUYA-KU
GINZA
78
YOYOGI
28
HARAJUKU
38
KOTO-KU
SHIBUYA EAST
14
AOYAMA
52
ROPPONGI AND AZABU-JUBAN
64
SHIBUYA WEST
XVI
DAIKANYAMA
180
EBISU
170
NAKAMEGURO
192
MINATO-KU
MEGURO AND GAKUGEI-DAIGAKU
204
MEGURO-KU
東京
TOKYO
SHINAGAWA-KU
OTA-KU

Maneki neko
(lucky cat)

Washi tapes & papers
(patterned paper tapes and
traditionally made paper)

Sake glasses & sets

Fans
(in paper, bamboo and wood)

Tea pots & cups

Mount Fuji anything!

Kitchenware

Kokeshi dolls
(traditional wooden dolls)

Geta
(clogs)

Sushi knives

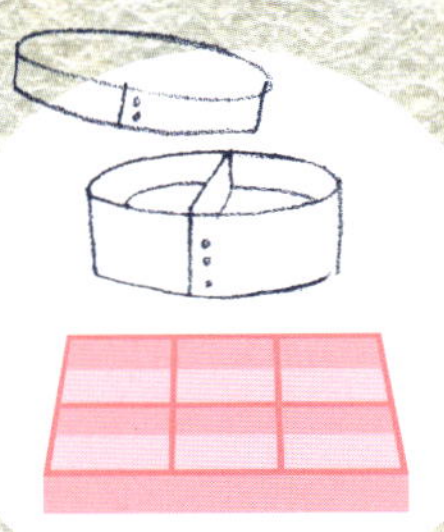

Bento boxes

Kimonos & Japanese fabrics

Toy robots

Calligraphy brushes

Capsule toys

Chopsticks & chopstick holders

Origami paper

Furoshiki
(beautiful fabric used
to wrap presents)

FOOD TO TRY IN TOKYO

Ramen
(wheat noodle soup, usually
made with pork broth)

Tempura
(battered and deep-fried
vegetables)

Taiyaki
(fish-shaped pastry filled with
bean paste or custard)

Tonkatsu
(deep-fried crumbed pork cutlet)

Kaiseki
(traditional multi-course,
seasonal cuisine)

Yakitori
(grilled meat and vegetables
on a skewer)

Japanese curry
(vegetable or meat curry served
over rice or noodles)

Takoyaki
(fried octopus balls)

Udon
(wheat flour noodles, served
chilled or in a hot fish and
seaweed broth)

Oden
(vegetables, fish cakes and egg
stewed in broth)

Unagi
(eel)

Nabe
(vegetables and/or meat and
noodles in a hotpot with mostly soy,
miso or seaweed stock)

Mochi & daifuku
(rice cakes with sweet filling)

Dango
(sweet rice-flour dumplings)

Matcha (maccha) ice-cream
(green tea ice-cream)

Soba
(buckwheat noodles served
chilled or in a hot fish and
seaweed broth)

Onigiri
(rice triangle wrapped in seaweed)

Sushi & sashimi
(cooked rice, often served
with seaweed, vegetables
and raw fish)

DRINKS TO TRY IN TOKYO

Coffee & coffee jelly

Sake: dry, sweet & sparkling
(alcohol from fermented rice)

Season beers & craft beers

Vending machine drinks
(green tea, juice, coffee,
alcohol and other drinks)

Ume shu
(plum wine)

Kuromame cha
(black soy bean tea)

Shochu
(alcohol distilled from barley,
buckwheat, sweet potato or rice)

Green teas, matcha, ocha,
hojicha & genmaicha
(a variety of green teas; genmaicha is green tea
combined with roasted brown rice)

Matcha latte
(green tea with milk, served
hot or cold)

自由席
NON-RESERVED
.門 司 港.
FOR MOJIKŌ
（大鳥神社角）
元気ハツラツ！
名種ビタミン・アミノ酸添加
オロナミン
C
ドリンク
炭酸飲料
大塚製薬
S

讀
讀
賣
新

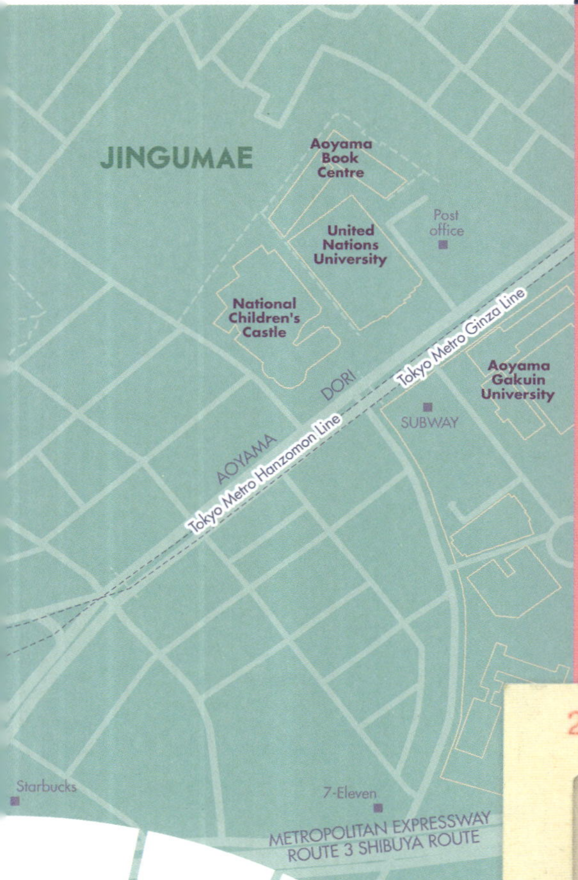

SHIBUYA WEST

With its neon flashing lights, giant TV screens and impossible crowds, Shibuya West cemented its pop-culture status long before the world came to snap pictures of it. This is an up-late precinct with a serious shopping addiction, and a bubbling laboratory where worldwide trends, youth fashion and lifestyles are born.

You'll find everything that's anything here, from seedy love hotels and games parlours to some of the world's best music venues, blockbuster art and oh, did we mention shopping?

SHOP

1 Shibuya Shopping
2 Grimoire
3 Wrapple
4 Postalco

EAT

5 Tokyu Food Show

EAT AND DRINK

6 Tofu Cuisine Sorano
7 Akiyoshi Yakitori
8 Suzu Cafe
9 Attic Room

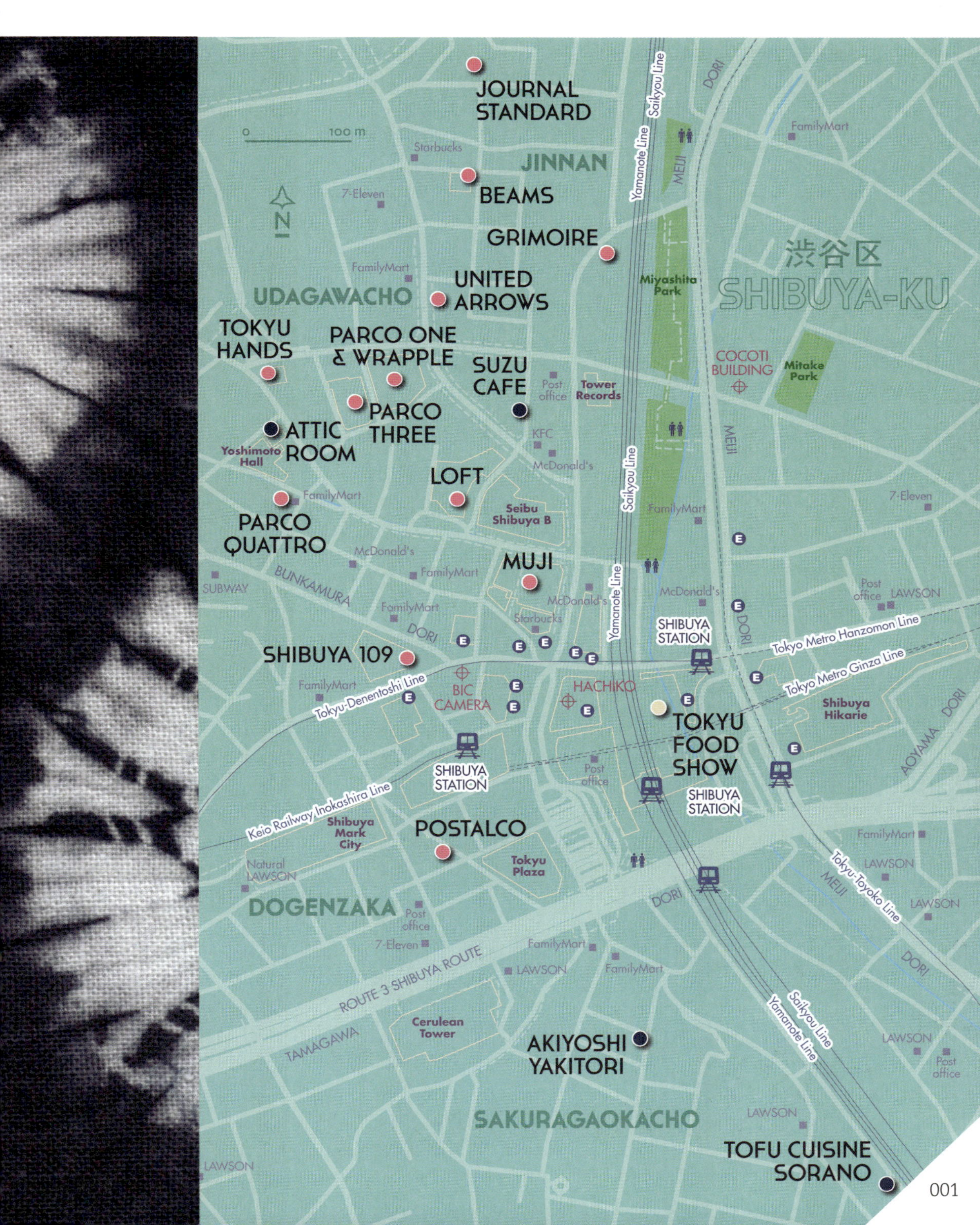
JOURNAL STANDARD
JINNAN
BEAMS
GRIMOIRE
UNITED ARROWS
UDAGAWACHO
TOKYU HANDS
PARCO ONE & WRAPPLE
SUZU CAFE
ATTIC ROOM
PARCO THREE
Yoshimoto Hall
LOFT
PARCO QUATTRO
MUJI
SUBWAY
SHIBUYA 109
BIC CAMERA
HACHIKO
TOKYU FOOD SHOW
POSTALCO
DOGENZAKA
Shibuya Mark City
Natural LAWSON
Tokyu Plaza
Cerulean Tower
AKIYOSHI YAKITORI
SAKURAGAOKACHO
TOFU CUISINE SORANO
渋谷区
SHIBUYA-KU
COCOTI BUILDING
Mitake Park
Miyashita Park
MEIJI
Yamanote Line
Saikyou Line
DORI
FamilyMart
Starbucks
7-Eleven
FamilyMart
Post office
Tower Records
KFC
McDonald's
Seibu Shibuya B
FamilyMart
McDonald's
FamilyMart
Starbucks
McDonald's
SHIBUYA STATION
Tokyo Metro Hanzomon Line
Tokyo Metro Ginza Line
Shibuya Hikarie
LAWSON
Post office
SHIBUYA STATION
SHIBUYA STATION
Keio Railway Inokashira Line
Tokyu-Denentoshi Line
FamilyMart
Post office
FamilyMart
FamilyMart
7-Eleven
LAWSON
ROUTE 3 SHIBUYA ROUTE
TAMAGAWA
BUNKAMURA DORI
AOYAMA DORI
MEIJI DORI
Tokyu-Toyoko Line
Saikyou Line
Yamanote Line
FamilyMart
LAWSON
LAWSON
LAWSON
Post office
Post office
7-Eleven
FamilyMart
0   100 m
N

SHIBUYA SHOPPING

See map

Nobody does shopping like Tokyo, and Shibuya West is definitely the precinct to see what's in and what's out. A good place to start is at the **Shibuya 109** building, an absolute fashion mecca, especially for the younger set. Get ideas on the latest styles from the kids on the street and then head into the fashion madhouse within 109 to put your look together. Parco is a group of department stores full of boutiques. **Parco One** has a selection of international and Japanese labels including chic bag-maker **Porter**, edgy designer **Tsumori** and a Japanese edition of sharp UK label **Fred Perry**. For those looking for fun, the wide-eyed doll Blythe shows off her wardrobe at **Junie Moon** (*see also* p. 185), and there's a mess of toys and anime at **Village Vanguard**. On the ground floor of Parco One is the fabulous **Parco Book Center**, a must for anyone hunting out Tokyo's best fashion, art and craft books. **Parco Three** is a youth fashion mecca with a more indie feel than 109. **Parco Quattro** is more about street style (and you can even catch bands playing live on the fifth floor). In the quiet backstreets, Tokyo stalwarts **Beams**, **United Arrows** and **Journal Standard** showcase some of Japan's best fashion. **Tokyu Hands** is a famous do-it-yourself megastore (*see also* p. 124), while conjoined stores **Muji** and **Loft** (*see also* p. 090) have inspiring homewares, stationery and lifestyle goods. It's all enough to keep even the most savvy shopper occupied for days!

PARCO
TOKYO TIP
Alleys and lanes hold
charming eateries, little
pockets of calm amongst
the madness.
PARCO

GRIMOIRE

8F, Ohata Building,
1-10-7 Jinnan, Shibuya-ku
3780 6203
www.grimoire-onlineshop.com
Open Mon–Fri 1–8pm,
Sat–Sun 12–8pm
Shibuya station, Hachiko exit

Grimoire will make you feel like you've dropped through the rabbit hole into the darkest parts of Wonderland to go vintage hunting with Alice. This sinister fairy forest caters to followers of the dolly-kei style, a mashup of Victorian lace, Grimm's fairytales and Gothic romance. Taxidermy, cuckoo clocks, creepy dolls, renaissance paintings and hanging puppets all conspire to make this the haunted house of retro shopping. Search the bulging racks of frou-frou dresses, Eastern European folk clothing and goth-girl cute for finds that are way outside the box. Embroidered trimmings, floral headpieces, cameos, brooches, patterned tights and Victorian perfume bottles complete the look.

WRAPPLE

4F, Shibuya Parco Part 1,
15-1 Udagawacho, Shibuya-ku
5428 8284
Open Mon–Sun 10am–9pm
Shibuya station, Hachiko exit

Ride the escalator to Parco One's (*see* p. 002) fourth floor and be greeted by a brightly coloured papier-mâché giraffe and cat standing guard over this mecca for craft and paper lovers. An almost endless array of washi (patterned paper tape), beautiful paper, bags, boxes, ribbons and string sits comfortably alongside retro, inspiring and utterly unexpected craft supplies. Ask about its workshops with local artists, where you can stick, cut, staple, glue and stamp your way to DIY paper heaven. At some stage you'll need a time-out at the Hutte coffee stand next door to devise ways to cram your purchases into your already overflowing suitcase.

POSTALCO

3F, Yamaji Building,
1-6-3 Dogenzaka, Shibuya-ku
6455 0531
http://postalco.net
Open Mon & Wed–Sat
12–8pm, Sun 12–6pm
Shibuya station, Inokashira line,
West exit

Found in a mega-stylish backstreet, Postalco makes some of the most beautiful leather products you are likely to find *anywhere*. Owners Mike and Yuri sell handcrafted versions of everyday items including wallets, bags, purses, cardholders, belts and even rainwear. Their collaborations with sought-after labels like Arts & Science (*see* p. 058), Opening Ceremony and Issey Miyake have cemented Postalco's place amongst Tokyo's design elite. Your credit card won't escape unscathed here, but each product is something that you'll value for life.

POSTALCO

5.

TOKYU FOOD SHOW

2-24-1 Dogenzaka, Shibuya-ku
3477 3111
www.tokyu-dept.co.jp/toyoko/
foodshow
Open Mon–Sun 10am–8pm
Shibuya station, Hachiko exit

You'll never think of shopping-centre food halls in the same way again after spending a few hours gawking at the variety of food on display in this basement hawkers' market. It's crazy at any time of the day, but things really get crowded when work is over and Tokyoites want to grab something to take home. The offerings run from Japanese and international street food to upmarket fare. Even the fussiest of eaters will be happy here, as there's just so much to choose from, including a great gyoza (dumpling) stand, rice-cracker stalls, sweets vendors and all manner of sushi, sashimi, grilled meats and rice dishes. There are free samples galore so you can try before you buy. Hit the food hall at closing time for some seriously marked-down bargains.

TOKYO TIP
Use one of the refrigerated lockers in Tokyu Food Show's food hall to store your purchases if you want to keep shopping!

TOFU CUISINE SORANO

4-17 Sakuragaokacho,
Shibuya-ku
5728 5191
Open Mon–Sun 5–11pm
Shibuya station, East exit

People who have spent their lives proclaiming that they hate tofu will eat their words at Tofu Cuisine Sorano. Dishes like the creamy, rich avocado tofu or crispy fried yuba (tofu skin) chips will likely convert the most die-hard tofu opponent. You'll find the restaurant on a narrow street alongside the train tracks. Head inside to its Zen-like interior and follow the pebble path past water features to one of the semi-private tatami rooms. It's fun to request the fresh tofu, which makes the journey from soy milk to tofu at your table. Most dishes come in at under ¥1000, while the eclectic drinks list includes beverages for around ¥600 (be adventurous and try the delicious soy cocktail or the sake cocktail with apricot pieces). Tofu even extends to dessert; the tiramisu and cheesecake are wickedly good. And if you still stand by your tofu-loathing words, never fear: there's plenty here for meat lovers too (the deep-fried black-bean chicken gets a thumbs up from us).

AKIYOSHI YAKITORI
17-12 Sakuragaokacho,
Shibuya-ku
3464 1518
Open Mon–Fri 5–11pm
Shibuya station, East exit

To find Akiyoshi Yakitori, look for the red lantern sign and wooden bench out the front. Get here early, as it's always packed out. You'll be greeted by hearty cries of 'irasshai!' (welcome!) as you head down into the noisy yakitori den. Choose a bar seat and settle in to watch the chefs in action. Standing behind a wall of smoke and flames, they grill some of the most delicious meat skewers imaginable (you'll be dreaming about them long after you've left). An English menu helps with the selection from the great range of yakitori staples. Yes, the grilled chicken here is a stand-out, but the agedashi (deep-fried) tofu is fantastic, as are the crumbed quail eggs and fried potatoes. Complement the excellent food with beer, sake or shochu (a distilled spirit), as you bump elbows with the locals and salarymen.

8.

SUZU CAFE

3F, Gems Building,
1-20-5 Jinnan, Shibuya-ku
5428 3739
Open Sun–Thurs 11.30am–
11.30pm, Fri–Sat 11.30am–2am
Shibuya station, Hachiko exit

This cosy third-floor cafe with a hotchpotch of vintage and modern industrial furniture is a quiet haven in the heart of busy Shibuya. Lunching shoppers and kids on dates are its main clientele, here to take advantage of the good-value lunch sets (¥1000; available from 11.30am to 3pm). You can opt for either the special red rice or a pasta dish; ask for the English menu. Curries and sandwiches cost even less and a beer will only tack a paltry ¥300 onto your bill. Eleven different desserts will give you the energy you need to continue your retail odyssey. When you've shopped till you've dropped, you can pop back in the evening, when candlelight, an extensive cocktail menu and an all-you-can-drink deal (¥2000 for two hours) provide the perfect conditions in which to unwind.

ATTIC ROOM

3F & 4F, 31-1 Udagawacho,
Shibuya-ku
5489 5228
Open Mon 5pm–12am,
Tues–Sun 12pm–12am
Shibuya station, Hachiko exit

If you're in need of a pick-me-up after shopping in the Tokyu Hands megastore, head to this cosy cafe just minutes away from the action. As the name suggests, the upstairs rooms resemble converted attic spaces complete with scattered toys, plants and eccentric objects like mailboxes. Vintage couches, found furniture, whitewashed walls and built-in hidey-holes complete the look. Try and get one of the cute cubbyhouse rooms; they only fit two people and are perfect for sweethearts or best friends. This is a good spot to lunch with the Shibuya set; rustic Asian-fusion dishes with a coffee, tea or juice will only set you back ¥1200. It's licensed, so it's also a great place for a late-night drink after you've finished hitting the shops.

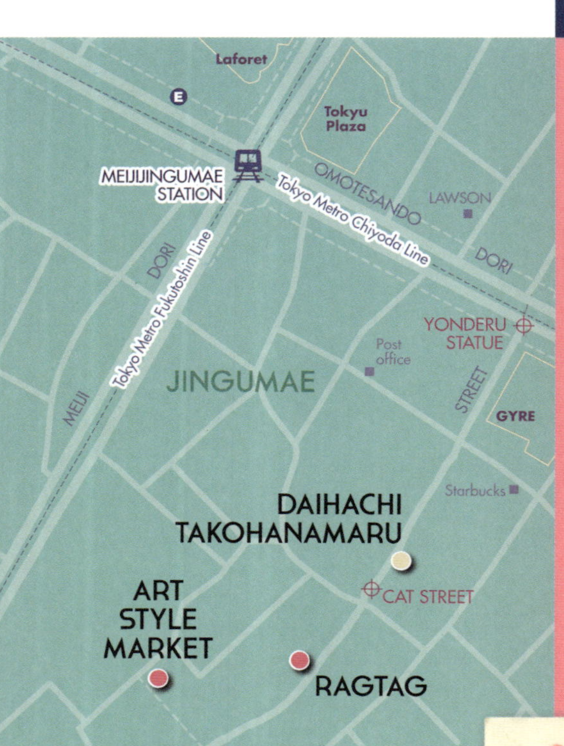

The east side of Shibuya is the opposite of the frenzied west (*see* p. xvi). Languid Cat Street is a great place for a lazy stroll on your way to Harajuku. Elsewhere, a thriving network of backstreets hides some of Shibuya's best eating and vintage-shopping opportunities.

Coffee stands seem to sprout daily and you'll also find edgy new fashion boutiques alongside Tokyo stalwarts. New kid on the block Hikarie, a towering department store, has brought a gentrified feel to Shibuya station's east side.

SHIBUYA EAST

SHOP

1 Sot
2 Art Style Market
3 Ragtag

SHOP AND EAT

4 Hikarie

EAT

5 Satei Hato
6 Daihachi Takohanamaru

EAT AND DRINK

7 Honoji
8 Nonbei Yokocho

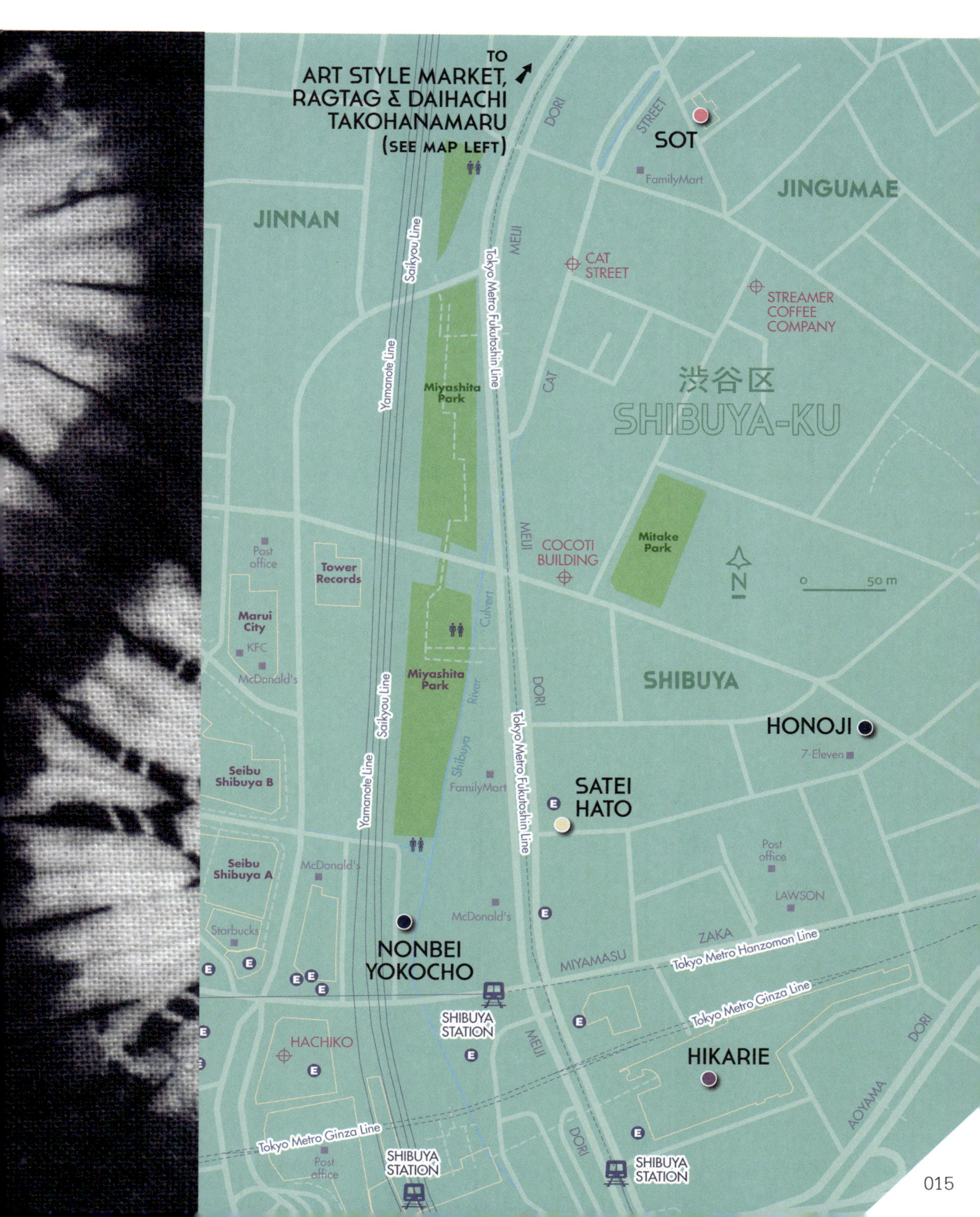

TO
ART STYLE MARKET,
RAGTAG & DAIHACHI
TAKOHANAMARU
(SEE MAP LEFT)
SOT
FamilyMart
JINGUMAE
JINNAN
Saikyou Line
Tokyo Metro Fukutoshin Line
MEIJI
CAT
STREET
CAT STREET
STREAMER COFFEE COMPANY
渋谷区
SHIBUYA-KU
Miyashita Park
Mitake Park
MEIJI
COCOTI BUILDING
N
0   50 m
Post office
Tower Records
SHIBUYA
Marui City
KFC
McDonald's
Miyashita Park
Shibuya River
Culvert
DORI
HONOJI
7-Eleven
Seibu Shibuya B
Saikyou Line
FamilyMart
SATEI HATO
Yamanote Line
Tokyo Metro Fukutoshin Line
Post office
LAWSON
Seibu Shibuya A
McDonald's
McDonald's
ZAKA
Starbucks
NONBEI YOKOCHO
MIYAMASU
Tokyo Metro Hanzomon Line
SHIBUYA STATION
Tokyo Metro Ginza Line
HACHIKO
MEIJI
HIKARIE
DORI
AOYAMA
Tokyo Metro Ginza Line
Post office
SHIBUYA STATION
DORI
SHIBUYA STATION
Yamanote Line

SOT

5-28-7 Jingumae, Shibuya-ku
5464 3677
Open Mon–Fri 12–8pm,
Sat–Sun 11.30am–8pm
Meiji-Jingumae station, exit 4

Mikami Tomohiro has put his own personality into this Shibuya branch of leather-goods maker Sot. The store is a beautiful little handicraft haven just off Cat Street decorated with found furniture, tiny illustrations and wooden slab tables. You can instantly see the quality of the leather goods for sale here. Bags and shoes feature prominently, including wonderfully wrinkled shoulder totes and stylishly distressed leather footwear, which add creativity to the everyday. You can also pick up folios, wallets and a wide range of intricate creations, such as the 'multipurpose leather case', a round coin purse that you can hang from your bag. Prices are on the high side, but that's what you have to pay for quality these days, and quality is what you'll find here.

TOKYO TIP
Check cafe opening hours in this neighbourhood, as many don't open until 11am or later.

ART STYLE MARKET

6-14-10 Jingumae, Shibuya-ku
3486 4875
Open Mon–Sun 11am–8pm
Meiji-Jingumae station, exit 4

You'll need to stroll around the hidden network of lanes off Cat Street to find Art Style Market. Located in its own peaceful enclave, this store will appeal to anyone partial to minimalist furniture, retro curios, mid-twentieth-century ornaments and kitchenalia. The furniture is on the industrial/medical side, with massive lights, metal tables, medical trolleys, stepladders and trestle tables. Paraphernalia addicts will love the out-there collection of wooden birds, buckets, glassware, spectacles, clocks, coffee makers, African masks and Thunderbirds figurines. There's a hint of the scientific here too, with shelves of glass beakers and test tubes that will take you straight back to your high-school chemistry class. If you don't fancy doing any dangerous experiments, these make great vases.

RAGTAG

6-14-2 Jingumae, Shibuya-ku
6419 3770
www.ragtag.jp
Open Mon–Sun 11am–8pm
Meiji-Jingumae station, exit 3

If you have a penchant for designer labels but shy away from their associated price tags, then this prominent Cat Street store could be your idea of shopping heaven. Ragtag stocks recycled clothes from all the best labels at marked-down prices. There are real bargains to be had on mid-range Japanese labels like A Bathing Ape and United Arrows on the ground floor. On the next floor up, snaffle some super deals on women's and men's high-end labels. You'll find top pieces by Chanel, Burberry and Marc Jacobs amongst many others. The top floor is for cleaning and repairs, or you can take your own designer cast-offs here and swap them for some yen – which you'll probably then go and spend downstairs.

4.

HIKARIE

2-21-1 Shibuya, Shibuya-ku
5468 5892
www.hikarie.jp
Open Mon–Sun 10am–9pm (department store);
Mon–Sun 11am–11pm (restaurants)
Shibuya station, exit 15

Sleek Shibuya newcomer Hikarie has managed to get some of Tokyo's best design retailers, galleries, cafes and restaurants under one roof. Kickstart your retail odyssey with a coffee at **Cream of the Crop**, then head straight to chic **ShinQs**. Your credit card is in for a definite work-out at this department store within a department store. ShinQs' self-proclaimed 'shopping for grown-ups' is an antidote to the plethora of Shibuya youth stores. Just about every style and genre is represented under its banner, and following are just a few of many places that stand out. Check out **Katakana** and **Bleu Bleuet** for kawaii (cute) gifts, and **Smith** for the latest retro-inspired gadgetry. Japanese artist Yayoi Kusama's avant-garde art is used on mugs and upscale novelties at the concept store **Lammfromm**. **Collex**, **Idée** and **Claska** all have unique and beautiful everyday household items that you can't possibly leave Tokyo without.

Design guru **D&Department** (*see also* p. 222) commands much of the 8th-floor space. This store elevates workaday items to things of beauty, and its gallery has regular shows that illuminate the high standards of Japanese design and handmade craft. Grab lunch or a coffee at D&Department's cafe, which has sensational views. Other food options await in the **food hall** on the two basement levels (great for takeaway) and on floors six and seven, where it's more about sit-down dining. A parting note: if it's raining outside, you can use the Shibuya station overpass to access Hikarie and all the treasures that lay within.

5.

SATEI HATO

1-15-19 Shibuya, Shibuya-ku
3400 9088
Open Mon–Sun 11am–11.30pm
Shibuya station, East exit

Kissaten (classic coffee houses) were all over Japan in the '50s and '60s, but now they're relatively few and far between. When you step into the kissaten Satei Hato, the world outside ceases to exist and time stands still. Its interior is a mishmash of European antiques, dark wood and Chinese designs, and low lighting and classical music add to the days-of-yore allure. You won't get latte art here, but you will get a warm welcome from genial host Toyoshi Taguchi, who's been working at Satei Hato since 1989. Grab a seat at the bar and he'll choose a cup to suit your personality from the great wall of china behind him. You'll be mesmerised as you watch him make your coffee – it's like witnessing a master craftsman in action. Order the chiffon cake with maple icing for a superb accompaniment to your brew. You're paying for the perfect blend in an exquisite cup in a beautiful setting here – so the coffee is a little more pricey than usual at ¥600 to ¥1000 per cup – but it's worth it for this thoroughly unique Tokyo experience.

6.

DAIHACHI TAKOHANAMARU

5-11-3 Jingumae, Shibuya-ku
3409 8787
Open Mon–Sun 12–9pm
Meiji-Jingumae station, exit 4

If you want to snack like a Tokyoite, line up at this Cat Street stand for some takoyaki, battered and fried octopus tentacles sprinkled with bonito flakes. It might not sound like the most appetising of snacks, but it's actually a Japanese staple akin to the Western sandwich, sausage roll or meat pie. The food stall is easily spotted by its orange lanterns and squid painted on the walls, which make it one of the most photographed spots on this strip. Get yourself a plate of these babies and add some pickles, green onion or mayo to jazz things up. Most people find they actually like the tasty little treats, and they're a great way to fuel up for a shopping frenzy in nearby Omotesando.

7.

HONOJI

1-11-3 Shibuya, Shibuya-ku
3407 4430
Open Mon–Sat
11.30am–2.30pm &
5.30–11pm
Shibuya station, exit 13

Local Tokyo comes alive at this izakaya in a quiet Shibuya backstreet. It's just a short walk from the bustling action, but once inside you'll feel miles away from anywhere. The interior is charming with its tatami mats and hanging paper menus written in kanji, and the food is excellent, simple pub grub, Japanese-style. Sizzling yakitori (grilled skewered meat), fresh sashimi and crispy gyoza dumplings demand to be washed down with a sake or two. It's a cheap and very cheerful place to grab a lunch set, but at night the charm steps up a notch. The evening banquet only costs ¥2500. Add ¥1500 to the bill for a two-hour, all-you-can-drink session and you're in for one of the best nights out in this fine town.

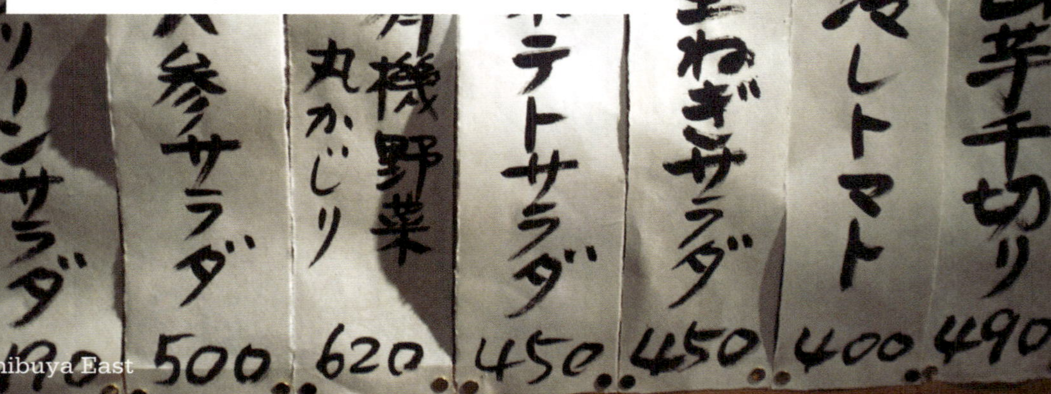

TOKYO TIP

Bic Camera is your one-stop electronics shop, with over five floors of cameras, gadgets and accessories.

6.

7.

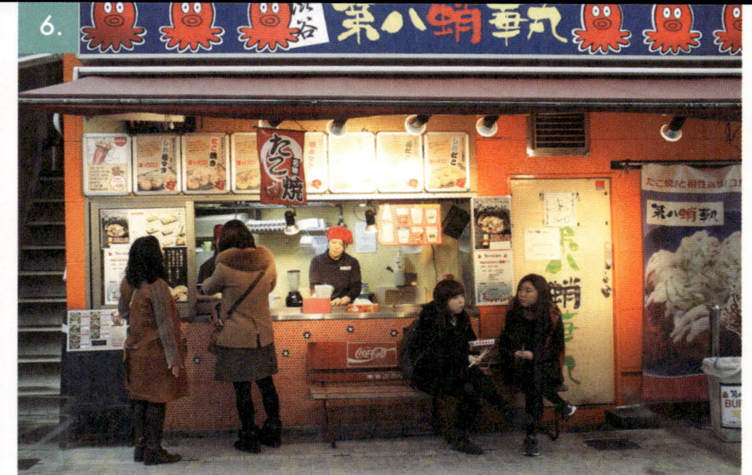

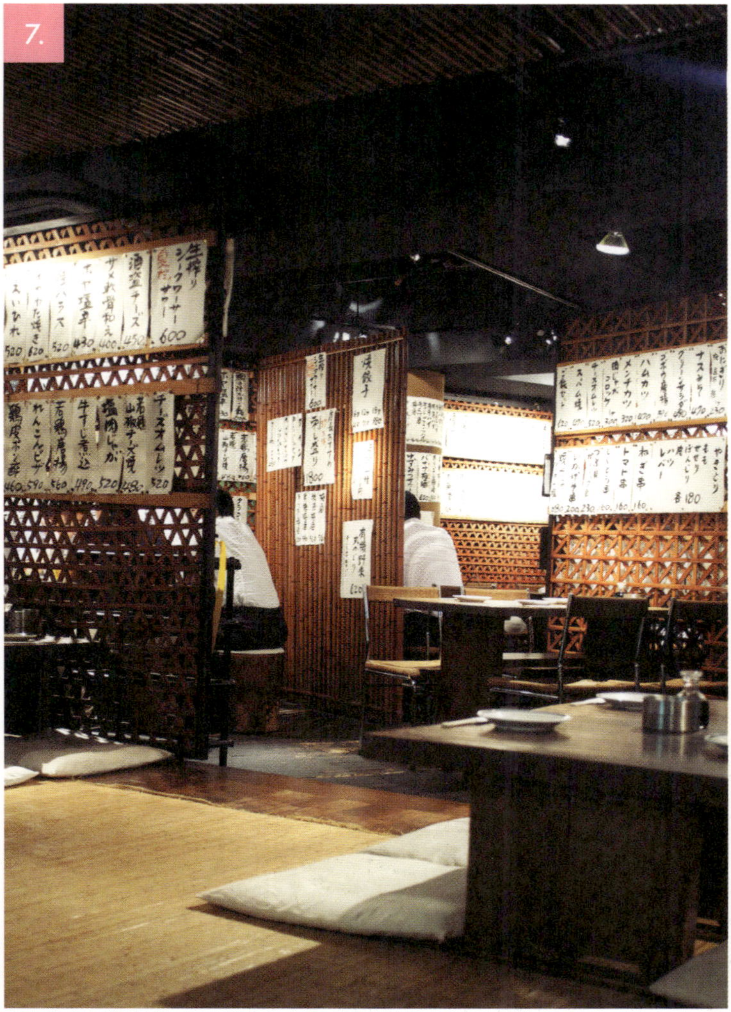

NONBEI YOKOCHO

Shibuya station, Hachiko exit
See map

Slip off the main drag in Shibuya to find Nonbei Yokocho, a shanty town of teeny-tiny bars squeezed into two beautiful lantern-lit alleyways. Some of the quaint little bars hold a total of only six people at a time. Others are spread over two floors, but even at these bigger places the most petite person will wonder if they'll be able to squeeze up the poky staircases. Drinking and stories are what you are here for and each bar has plenty of both. There's excellent food as well: **Torishige**, a yakitori (grilled skewered meat) restaurant, rates a special mention. Nonbei is slang for 'drunkard', so don't be shy – squash yourself into this delightful Tokyo time warp and get a few drinks into you.

TOKYO TIP
Many of Nonbei Yokocho's bars don't have toilets, so you'll have to brave the public facilities outside.

Mikami Tomohiro owns Sot (*see* p. 016), the leather-goods store just off Cat Street. He likes to be called Tomo by his friends, and loves art, illustration and vintage furniture.

How important is craftsmanship in Japanese design?

For great leather making, craftsmanship is absolutely essential. It's the most important thing for my store, and a big part of why Japan produces such high-quality, timeless products.

What is your favourite piece in your shop?

My favourite item is the 'multipurpose leather case'. It is crafted into a cute, round shape and has a hook; it looks great hanging from your favourite bag.

Where do you like to drink coffee in Shibuya?

I like the Streamer Coffee Company (*see* map p. 015), which is just a one-minute walk from my store. You can enjoy delicious coffee in big cups.

Where do you go for a quick escape from Tokyo?

You will find both the sea and the mountains in the area of Hayama, Kanagawa prefecture.

It's a great place to relax, very peaceful. On days of rest I go there often. It only takes about two hours to get there from Shibuya.

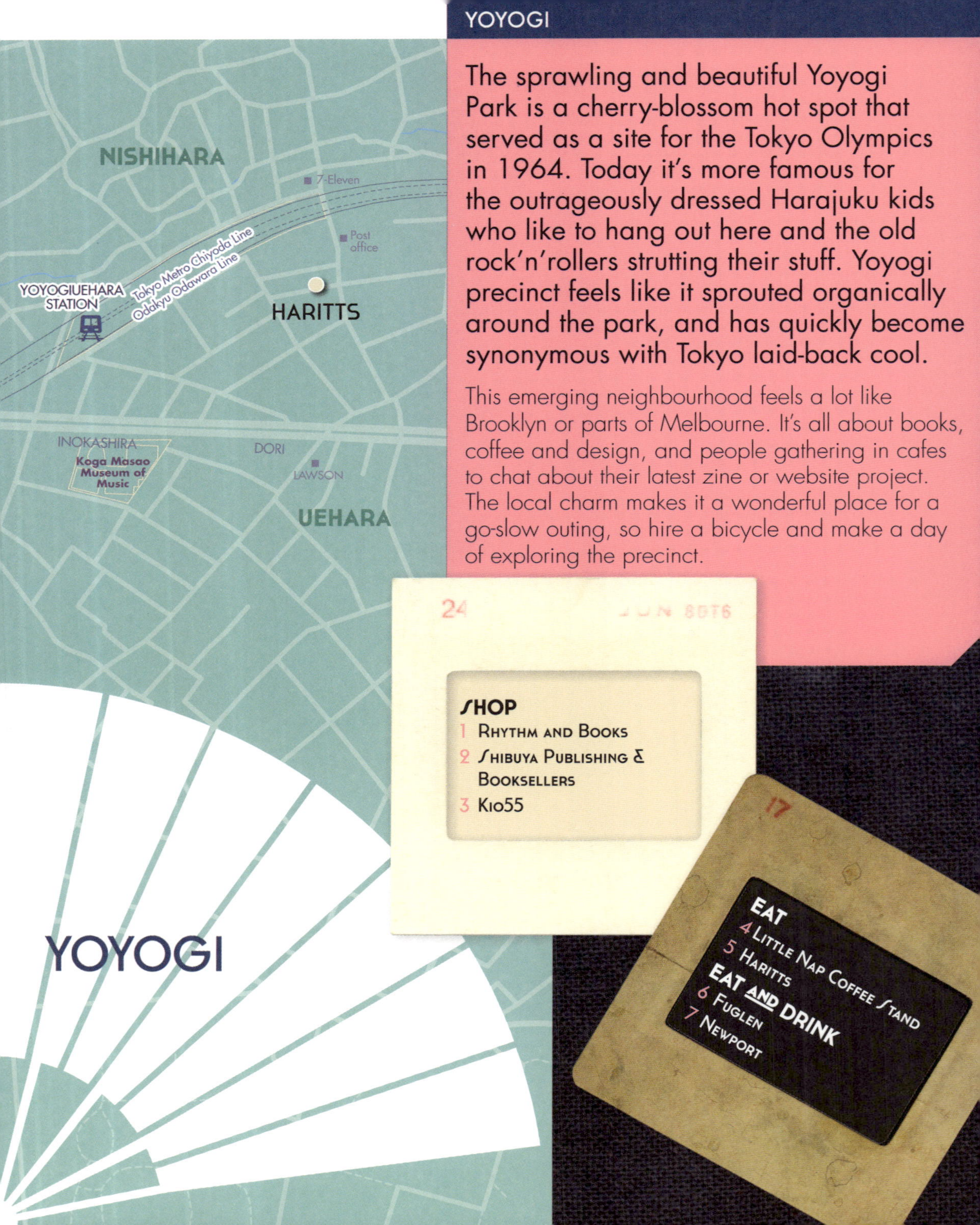

The sprawling and beautiful Yoyogi Park is a cherry-blossom hot spot that served as a site for the Tokyo Olympics in 1964. Today it's more famous for the outrageously dressed Harajuku kids who like to hang out here and the old rock'n'rollers strutting their stuff. Yoyogi precinct feels like it sprouted organically around the park, and has quickly become synonymous with Tokyo laid-back cool.

This emerging neighbourhood feels a lot like Brooklyn or parts of Melbourne. It's all about books, coffee and design, and people gathering in cafes to chat about their latest zine or website project. The local charm makes it a wonderful place for a go-slow outing, so hire a bicycle and make a day of exploring the precinct.

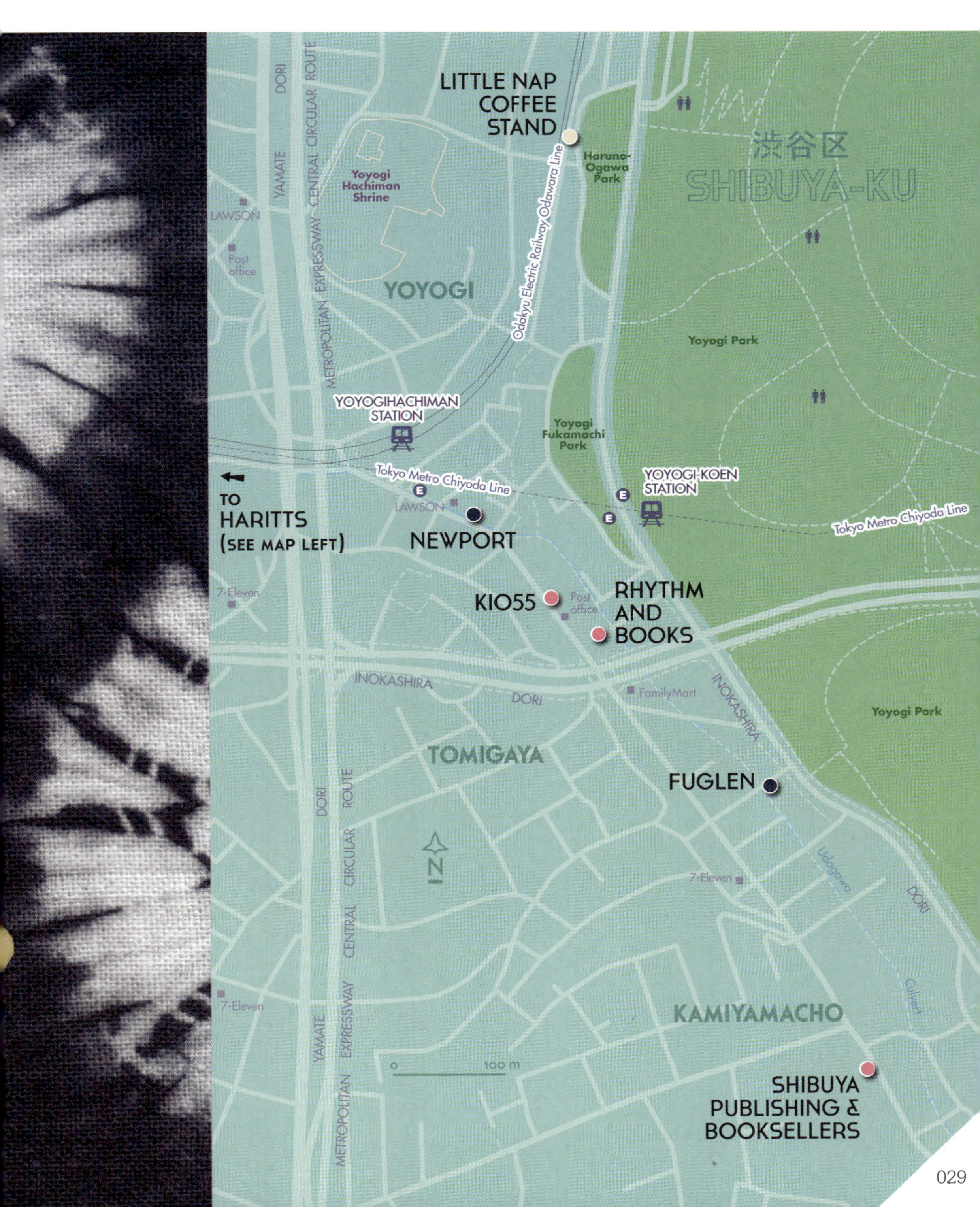

LITTLE NAP COFFEE STAND
Yoyogi Hachiman Shrine
YAMATE DORI
METROPOLITAN EXPRESSWAY CENTRAL CIRCULAR ROUTE
LAWSON
Post office
YOYOGI
Odakyu Electric Railway Odawara Line
Haruno-Ogawa Park
渋谷区 SHIBUYA-KU
Yoyogi Park
YOYOGIHACHIMAN STATION
Yoyogi Fukamachi Park
Tokyo Metro Chiyoda Line
YOYOGI-KOEN STATION
Tokyo Metro Chiyoda Line
TO HARITTS (SEE MAP LEFT)
LAWSON
NEWPORT
7-Eleven
KIO55
Post office
RHYTHM AND BOOKS
INOKASHIRA DORI
FamilyMart
INOKASHIRA
Yoyogi Park
TOMIGAYA
FUGLEN
YAMATE DORI
METROPOLITAN EXPRESSWAY CENTRAL CIRCULAR ROUTE
N
7-Eleven
Udagawa DORI
Culvert
7-Eleven
KAMIYAMACHO
0   100 m
SHIBUYA PUBLISHING & BOOKSELLERS

1.

RHYTHM AND BOOKS

1-9-15 Tomigaya, Shibuya-ku
6407 0788
Open Mon–Fri 12–10pm,
Sat–Sun 12–8pm
Yoyogi-Koen station, exit 2

Rhythm and Books is a tiny store jammed to the ceiling with retro books and music from Japan and Europe, all presided over by the dangling legs of a robot or two. You'll have to walk sideways like a crab to get through the skinny aisles, but the ramshackle collection of nostalgia here is artfully chosen and you're sure to unearth some real treasures. The postcards with hilarious hairstyles of '70s pop stars are a treat, but it's the great children's books, vintage Japanese magazines and novels with cool retro covers that make this place extra special.

2.

SHIBUYA PUBLISHING & BOOKSELLERS

17-3 Kamiyamacho, Shibuya-ku
5465 0588
Open Mon–Sat 12pm–2am,
Sun 12–10pm
Yoyogi-Koen station, exit 2

The good folk at Shibuya Publishing & Booksellers have such fine-tuned taste that what starts out as a quick flick through the material on offer usually turns into an extended scouring session. Shelves and trestle tables in this minimalist, relaxed store are stuffed with contemporary novels and magazines, but that's only half the story: the bookstore also fosters and publishes local would-be writers. You'll find comics, novellas, tracts and rants of all kinds gracing the stands, so you can get wise to what could be the next big thing in magazines or check out some edgy new manga. There are regular publishing workshops, and you can even rent out the in-store display box to peddle your zine or handmade stationery. It's open to 2am most nights, perfect for that late-night browse.

3.

KIO55

1-9-19 Tomigaya, Shibuya-ku
6804 9888
Open Mon–Fri 11am–6pm,
Sat 12–6pm
Yoyogi-Koen station, exit 2

Kio55 is a fantastic repository for the finest cooking and dining vessels; it stocks a beautiful range of kitchenware with a definite Scandinavian leaning. Designers are mostly unknown, which comes as a surprise given the fine quality of the bowls, plates, cutlery, carafes and enamelware on the shelves of the tiny, brightly lit store. Check out Tokyo designer Mutsumi's impressive wooden plate and bread knife, which somehow manages to be both traditional and futuristic at the same time. There's a selection of artfully arranged leather goods as well, including tote bags and purses. The entrance to the store is a little obscure, so keep your eyes peeled for the miniscule fish on a yellow board outside.

4

LITTLE NAP COFFEE STAND

5-65-4 Yoyogi, Shibuya-ku
3466 0074
www.littlenap.jp
Open Tues–Sun 9am–7pm
Yoyogi-Hachiman station, exit 3

Park your bicycle out the front of Little Nap and head into this coffee pit stop opposite Yoyogi Park. It's not so much a cafe as a hip shoebox, with Americana-style signage, big maps on the walls and bags of rustic charm. There are bags of coffee beans about the place too, as the owners roast their own. Seating is limited to a few stools inside and a bench outside, but no matter, as it's mostly about takeaway here. The excellent drip coffee and espresso have made this the go-to place for anyone finding themselves in need of a pick-me-up after a picnic and a little nap in the park. While you're here, join the peeps taking happy snaps on the bench out the front.

5.

HARITTS

1-34-2 Uehara, Shibuya-ku
3466 0600
Open Tues–Fri 8am–6pm,
Sat–Mon 11am–6pm
Yoyogi-Uehara station, exit 2

Haritts is not that easy to find, so look for the cute little doughnut board that marks the tiny side street the shop is on. Behind the sliding door of this charming old Japanese house, the owners have perfected the art of the handmade doughnut. Get in early for sought-after flavours like cinnamon raisin or cream cheese, as these delicious, sugary dough clouds have a habit of running out quickly. In fact, to keep things fair, customers are limited to five doughnuts each on weekdays, three on weekends! Even the basic doughnuts here are lip-smackingly good, especially when downed with Haritts's coffee, and the price is right at just ¥157 each.

TOKYO TIP
In the north-west part of Yoyogi Park you can hire bicycles for just ¥200 per hour.

FUGLEN

1-6-11 Tomigaya, Shibuya-ku
3481 0084
www.fuglen.no/japanese
Open Mon–Tues 8am–7pm,
Wed 8am–12am, Thurs
8am–1am, Fri 8am–2am, Sat
10am–2am, Sun 10am–12am
Yoyogi-Koen station, exit 2

- -

This Norwegian coffee house is perfectly at home in Yoyogi. Its interior is warm and inviting, with a '50s-slash-'60s modernist Japanese bent, and quality siphon coffee is served, making it a great place to start your day or relax on a lazy afternoon. Expect the benches to be propping up blonde models and Scandophiles, but other locals also flock here to unwind. Warm-wood shelves display ceramic pieces from top Scandinavian designers like Stig Lindberg and Lisa Larson and it's all for sale! At night Fuglen spills onto the street and morphs into an ultra-hip bar selling Norwegian and Japanese craft beers, and some very tempting cocktails.

NEWPORT

1-6-8 Tomigaya, Shibuya-ku
5738 5564
www.nwpt.jp
Open Mon–Fri 11.30am–
12am, Sat 12pm–12am
Yoyogi-Hachiman station, exit 3

Effortlessly put together Newport makes a great spot to stop for lunch, dinner or drinks when shopping in Yoyogi. It's probably the closest thing Tokyo has to a hip Brooklyn indie cafe. The small space is decked out with peeling posters, rustic furniture and blackboard menus listing dinner fare that's a mix of Americana, Mediterranean and European. Dishes are good for sharing and are well-priced at ¥520 to ¥1390 each. Lunch is usually a simplified version of the dinner plates; at around ¥1000 it's one of the best deals in town, and healthy to boot. As an added bonus, there's plenty here for vegetarians, including popular falafels.

At night it turns into a bar and is a great place to sink into a chair and relax with a glass of wine for just ¥550. On Saturday nights, the tiny DJ booth fires up so you can listen to some tunes while sharing a bottle of something.

Buzzing Harajuku has been reinventing itself as a youth destination since the 1920s. From the mad crush of pedestrian-only Takeshita Dori to the majestic sweep of Omotesando, a wide, tree-lined street reminiscent of a French boulevard, this is where young Tokyoites come to flaunt eye-popping fashion and queue for the newest cafe.

Omotesando is the epicentre of Harajuku. International brands vie for attention here, showcasing beautifully curated fashion in spectacular buildings created by a who's who of Japanese architects. Boasting a network of seriously fabulous backstreets, Harajuku holds the key to some of Tokyo's unmissable shopping and dining experiences.

N
0   100 m
Togo Shrine
7-Eleven
TAKESHITA DORI
Tokyo Metro Fukutoshin Line
DESIGN FESTA GALLERY
FamilyMart
Starbucks
MEIJI DORI
BIG LOVE RECORDS
Post office
Ryugenji Temple
GAIEN NISHI DORI
Natural LAWSON
TO OFFICE BAR
(SEE MAP LEFT)
Myoen Temple
SAKURA TEI OKONOMIYAKI
APC UNDERGROUND
FamilyMart
JINGUMAE
GAR EDEN
GALERIE DOUX DIMANCHE
Laforet
MEIJI DORI
Tokyu Plaza
MEIJIJINGUMAE STATION
LAWSON
CHICAGO INC
OMOTESANDO KOFFEE
7-Eleven
MAISEN
KIDDY LAND
Post office
GYRE
ORIENTAL BAZAAR
Starbucks
OMOTESANDO
Omotesando Hills
FamilyMart
OMOTESANDO DORI
Starbucks
ZENKOJI TEMPLE
LOUIS VUITTON
Tokyo Metro Chiyoda Line
OMOTESANDO DORI
SUBWAY
OMOTESANDO STATION
SHIBUYA
渋谷区
SHIBUYA-KU
KITA-AOYAMA
Starbucks
AOYAMA DORI
KFC

1.

KIDDY LAND

6-1-9 Jingumae, Shibuya-ku
3409 3431
www.kiddyland.co.jp
Open Mon–Fri 11am–9pm,
Sat–Sun 10.30am–9pm
Harajuku station, Omotesando
exit, or Meiji-Jingumae station,
exit 4

Kiddy Land is one of Tokyo's quintessential shopping experiences. It's a toy store like no other. Kids and kidults flock here for new fads and old favourites among the constantly evolving selections. Searching for limited-edition figurines? You'll get them here. Need a kimono for your Blythe fashion doll? No problem. Hello Kitty and Miffy obsessive? Sure thing! Star Wars headphones, character lunch boxes, crazy phone accessories: it's all here jam-packed into five mesmerising floors. Some of the store's best items can be nabbed for next to nothing, but the serious collector can go to town here as well. Its motto 'For the human smile' sums up how you will feel as you walk out of Kiddy Land with your stash.

2.

BIG LOVE RECORDS

3F, 2-31-3 Jingumae, Shibuya-ku
5775 1315
www.bigloverecords.jp
Open Mon 3–8pm,
Tues–Sun 1–10pm
Meiji-Jingumae station, exit 5

You have to go to the edge of Harajuku, down a random side street and up several flights of stairs to find Big Love Records, but it's oh-so worth it. This would have to be one of the coolest record stores/cafes/bars in the world. It's amazing what they pack into the small space here, with racks of great music squeezed between a bar that looks like a Mexican cantina and a tiny rustic cafe. The vinyl, zines and cassette tapes will take you back to the glory days of the '80s, but there are plenty of up-to-date international indie releases as well. The independent ethos extends to the bar's rotating crop of rare Japanese craft beers, which you can gulp down while listening to some truly select tunes.

SONIC YOUTH
tame
impala
TOY

TAPES Never Went Away
HIGHER PLANES
CAPTURED TRACKS
NIGHT-PEOPLE
SIXTEEN TAMBOURINES
THE GARDEN

BIG LOVE
RECORDS
HARAJUKU
TOKYO

tue - sun 1-10pm
mon 3 -8pm

3

APC UNDERGROUND

4-27-6 Jingumae, Shibuya-ku
5775 7216
Open Mon–Sun 12–8pm
Meiji-Jingumae station, exit 3

It's easy to see why Sofia Coppola wanted to use the APC Underground store for a scene in *Lost in Translation* – it's such a unique space. A small ex-storeroom, part spaceship and part futuristic cruise ship with its tiny porthole windows, the store is a modular pod tucked away on a fashionable backstreet off Omotesando. It isn't an easy find, but you'll be glad you walked down the stairs and crunched across the pebbles when you see the must-haves from the APC fashion collection, which incorporates beautiful tailoring, classic shapes and timeless French chic. It's worth seeking out limited-edition items too, like 2008's Harajuku bomber jacket. The staff are also on display here, effortlessly sharp in the latest range. Sizing is in French, and ranges from extra-small to large.

CHICAGO INC
4-26-26 Jingumae, Shibuya-ku
5414 5107
Open Mon–Sun 11am–8pm
Meiji-Jingumae station, exit 3

The vintage clothing boom has hit Tokyo with full force! And Chicago Inc's owners are spot on when it comes to trend forecasting. Whatever is coming into fashion, be it '70s hippy chic or '80s tartan, the original versions will be here minus the designer price tag. There are separate Japanese and American sections; the latter's aisles are brimming with pre-loved denim overalls, maxi-dresses, baseball and biker jackets, and Hawaiian shirts. Many of the items have a story to tell, especially the kimonos and obis (sashes) with their faded beauty. Sizes are on the small side, so they won't suit everyone, but there's a vast range of badges, belts, scarves and sunglasses so at the very least you can be gorgeously accessorised.

5.

GALERIE DOUX DIMANCHE

3-5-6 Jingumae, Shibuya-ku
3408 5120
www.2dimanche.com
Open Mon–Sun 12–7.30pm
Omotesando station, exit A2

It's easy to see owner Hisashi Tokuyoshi's love of all things French and Scandinavian in this craft oasis in a cosy backstreet, just minutes from Harajuku's chaotic core. Make no mistake though: Galerie Doux Dimanche is thoroughly Japanese in its aesthetic. The delightfully twee interior is a mini gallery with a handicraft store attached. Always turning the cute factor up to 11, the gallery shows works by local illustrators and artists, while the store has a colourful selection of French-style bric-a-brac, fabric, stationery and charming stuff to jazz up your kid's bedroom. In addition to the gallery and shop, the publisher **Paumes** is located upstairs. It produces small inspirational books and zines that explore the environments of creative people globally, and curates the exhibitions for the gallery downstairs.

TOKYO TIP
Hit the eight-floor Laforet
fashion mecca during
sales to witness some truly
over-the-top spruiking.

SAKURA TEI OKONOMIYAKI

3-20-1 Jingumae, Shibuya-ku
3479 0039
www.sakuratei.co.jp
Open Mon–Sun 11am–11pm
Meiji-Jingumae station, exit 3

Ever wanted to practise being a chef? Well here's your chance. Admittedly you'll only be making omelettes, but hey, Tokyo wasn't built in a day. Kids love it here, but make sure you keep their elbows (and yours!) off the accident-waiting-to-happen hotplate tables. Order a bowl of ingredients (English menus are available), throw everything onto the sizzling hotplate, add an egg, et voilà! The resulting mess is your very own Japanese omelette. It's cheap and tasty, and a lively mix of tourists and locals keeps the place buzzing, as does the well-stocked bar. After you've eaten, check out an exhibition at the attached **Design Festa Gallery**, a labyrinth of tiny rooms showing works by local artists.

MAISEN

4-8-5 Jingumae, Shibuya-ku
3470 0071
Open Mon–Sun 11am–10pm
Omotesando station, exit A2

To say Maisen is a Tokyo institution is a bit of an understatement. Legions of loyal followers, both local and international, make their way through Harajuku's winding backstreets to this famous tonkatsu joint to order the delicate pork in breadcrumbs. Join the queue (which can be long but moves quickly) and ask to be seated in the beautiful former bathhouse or the delightful traditional tatami room. Dishes range from excellent to awesome. The pinnacle of the menu is the black pork; smother it in one of Maisen's two signature 'secret' sauces (we prefer the thick, sweet plum one), then eat it with mounds of addictive shredded cabbage. One of the well-chosen sakes is the perfect way to wash it down. If you don't eat pork, there are also delicious prawn, salad and sashimi options. On your way out, make sure you buy some secret sauce to wow your friends back home.

6.

7.

TOKYO TIP
The wonderful gallery at
the top of the Louis Vuitton
building is free.

OMOTESANDO KOFFEE

4-15-3 Jingumae, Shibuya-ku
5413 9422
Open Mon–Sun 10am–9pm
Omotesando station, exit A2

Widely regarded (especially by us) as the best coffee in Tokyo, Omotesando Koffee is a minimalist wooden cube set in a small 60-year-old house. It's a little hard to find but it's worth the wander, especially if you happen to be rolling out of Maisen (*see* p. 046) around the corner in desperate need of a caffeine hit. Feel the love as you watch owner Eiichi Kunitomo work his magic on the La Cimbali coffee machine, giving your coffee that personal touch. The speciality here is espresso, but our preference is the creamy latte, which you can savour alongside delicious tiny baked custards. Feeling frisky? Try the Baileys cappuccino! You can take your coffee away, or enjoy it outside in the relaxing Zen courtyard.

OFFICE BAR

5F, Yamazaki Building,
2-7-18 Kita-Aoyama, Minato-ku
5786 1052
Open Mon–Sun 7pm–3am
Gaiemmae station, exit 3

As the name suggests, this 5th-floor bar used to be an office and a lot of what was formerly here has been incorporated into the bar's minimalist aesthetic, including a photocopier, fax machine, filing cabinets, lamps and desks. Needless to say, the atmosphere's a lot more relaxed in its current incarnation, but the free wi-fi, big tables and cubbyholes about the place still allow you to catch up on some work if need be. The view is amazing, the music chilled and the drinks are just what you need to shake off the thought of that encroaching deadline.

Coco Tashima was born and raised in Oita, but has lived in Tokyo since her university days. She edits and writes for Paumes (*see* p. 044), a Japanese publisher that produces inspirational books and zines. She loves good food and drink (and sometimes cooking), and strolling around.

How do you define Tokyo style?

For me, Tokyo's fashion is like a kaleidoscope. It's not always beautiful though. There are lots of very unique looks in different parts of Tokyo, reflecting the various characteristics of each precinct.

What is your favourite thing at Paumes?

It is difficult to choose one thing! You can find all of Paumes's books here. We have published over 70 titles already, and that number continues to grow. Every book is a precious treasure of our encounters with wonderful talented artists and designers. The books are always an inspiration and I am proud of them.

Where do you like to eat and drink in Harajuku?

In the Paumes neighbourhood, I like to go to Gar Eden (*see* map p. 039), an Italian restaurant. For lunch you can enjoy homemade pasta or a tasty meat dish. Its service is pleasant and attentive. It also has a great selection of craft beers.

Where do you go for a quick escape from Tokyo?

I can feel like I am escaping from Tokyo at Kinuta Park in Setagaya, even though it's in Tokyo! It's a large park with a lot of greenery and seasonal flowers. The lovely Setagaya Art Museum is also in the park.

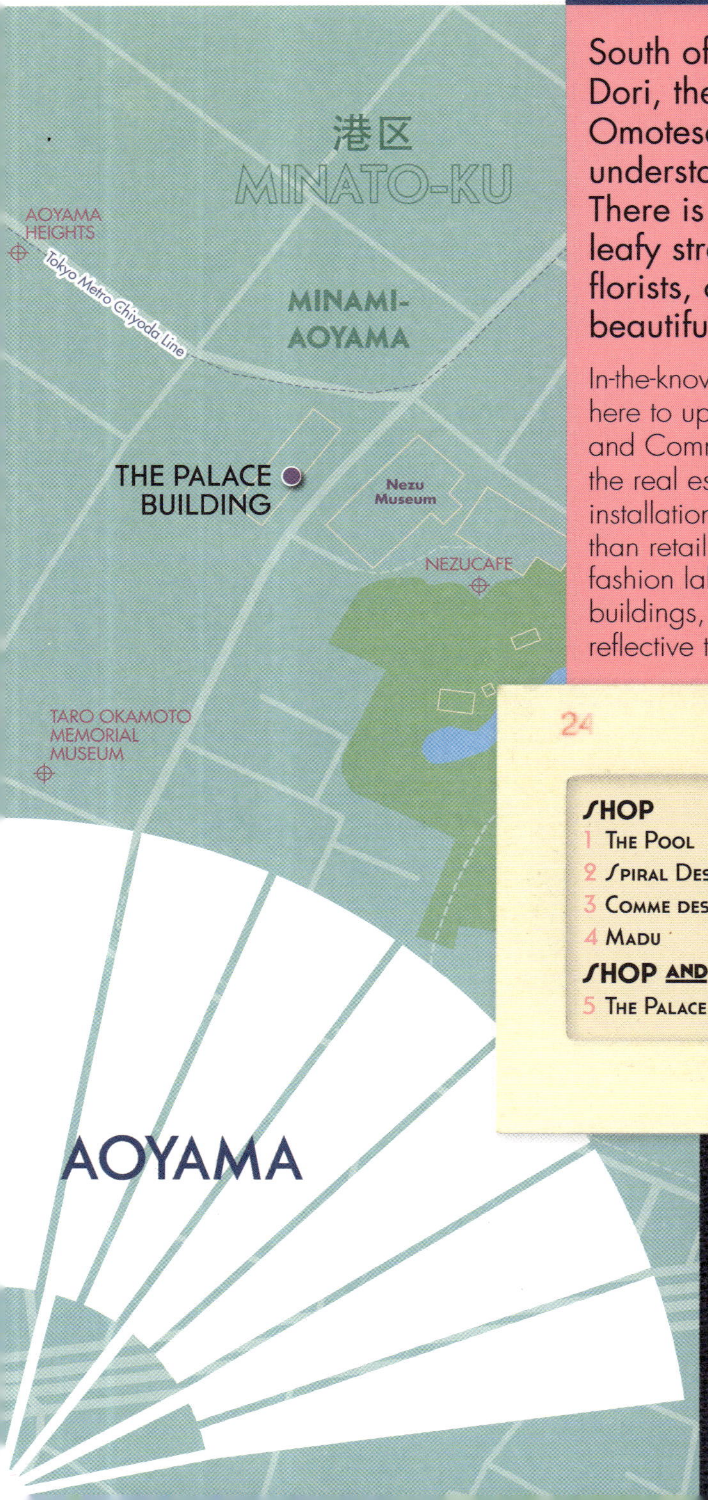

AOYAMA

South of the thoroughfare of Aoyama Dori, the madness of Harajuku and Omotesando gives way to chic, understated Tokyo style in Aoyama. There is an atmosphere of calm in these leafy streets lined with fashion boutiques, florists, organic cafes and stores selling beautiful handmade wares.

In-the-know international and local shoppers come here to update their wardrobes. Issey Miyake and Comme des Garçons command much of the real estate here, and statues, art projects and installations make the stores look more like galleries than retail outlets. Coveted Japanese and European fashion labels are housed in famous architectural buildings, brave new additions to the landscape of reflective temples, shrines and samurai houses.

SHOP
1 The Pool
2 Spiral Design Market
3 Comme des Garçons
4 Madu

SHOP AND EAT
5 The Palace Building

EAT
6 Gonbē
7 Aoyama Flower Market Tea House

EAT AND DRINK
8 A to Z Cafe

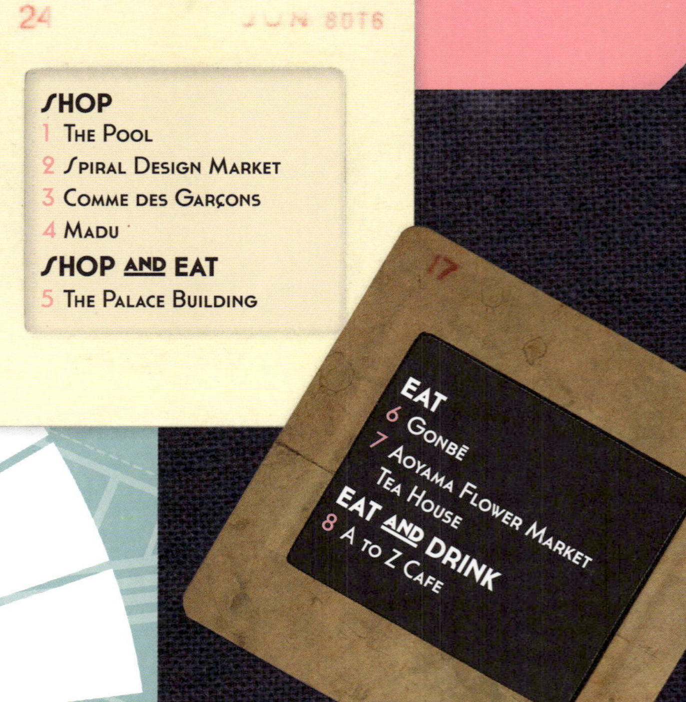

OMOTESANDO DORI
AOYAMA DORI
SUBWAY
Tokyo Metro Chiyoda Line
OMOTESANDO STATION
Starbucks
FamilyMart
AOYAMA FLOWER MARKET TEA HOUSE
ISSEY MIYAKE
COMME DES GARÇONS
Tokyo Metro Chiyoda Line
AOYAMA DORI
Tokyo Metro Ginza Line
Tokyo Metro Hanzomon Line
港区
MINATO-KU
SPIRAL DESIGN MARKET
TO THE PALACE BUILDING
(SEE MAP LEFT)
GONBĒ
MINAMI-AOYAMA
KOTTO
FamilyMart
Starbucks
MADU
A TO Z CAFE
0   50 m
Aoyama Gakuin University
FamilyMart
LAWSON
DORI
Starbucks
渋谷区
SHIBUYA-KU
THE POOL

1.

THE POOL

5-12-24 Minami-Aoyama,
Minato-ku
3746 2553
http://the-pool-aoyama.com
Open Mon–Sun 11am–8pm
Omotesando station, exit B1

The interior of this store is a striking rework of an old swimming pool that was formerly used by residents of a '70s apartment block. Even if swimming isn't your thing, you'll be entranced by the aquatic-related fashion here. Vintage elements lend charm to the cutting-edge swimwear and sci-fi poolside chic, while the store's glass floor makes you feel like you're walking on water while you shop. Dive in to see Tokyo retail at its contemporary best.

2.

SPIRAL DESIGN MARKET

5-6-23 Minami-Aoyama,
Minato-ku
3498 1171
www.spiral.co.jp
Open Mon–Sun 11am–8pm
Omotesando station, exit B1

Spiral Design Market is a design store, cafe, bar and gallery rolled into one. The snail-shell-shaped ramp that gives Spiral its name winds through a gallery space showing special exhibitions by emerging designers, architects, furniture makers, jewellers and artists. On the second floor you'll find a skillfully curated selection of homewares, which the store markets as 'simple products for everyday use'. The beautiful range is well priced, so you're sure to find something to style up your home. If not, check out the attached **Spiral Records**, which distills the vast selection of music available today into the hippest CDs from around the world.

TOKYO TIP
The eclectic Watari Museum of Contemporary Art is worth checking out.

3.

COMME DES GARÇONS

5-2-1 Minami-Aoyama,
Minato-ku
3406 3951
www.comme-des-garcons.com
Open Mon–Sun 11am–8pm
Omotesando station, exit A5

This flagship store for Comme des Garçons is a showroom that blurs the lines between art and retail. Designer Rei Kawakubo is the founder of the store and her tortured futurist kimonos and Gothic lace party dresses make the space feel more like a contemporary art exhibition than a fashion store. High-flyers with a taste for the edgy head to Comme to see if they can carry off Kawakubo's intricately engineered creations. They'll never look as good as the staff though, who float around the store like museum exhibits on a catwalk. If your budget doesn't stretch to a Comme des Garçons dress or jacket, you can always pick up one of its beautiful Japan-only fragrances or ubercool T-shirts for around ¥7000.

4.

MADU

5-8-1 Minami-Aoyama,
Mincto-ku
3498 2971
www.madu.jp
Open Mon–Sun 11am–8pm
Omotesando station, exit B1

You'll find this unpretentious gift and homewares store down a side street off Omotesando. It's not a souvenir shop, but the items – which are very Japanese, affordable and tastefully selected – are perfect for gifts or for prettying up your home. If you are looking for chopsticks, chopstick rests, linen, delicate glassware, teapots and incense, you'll find well-chosen and well-priced versions of them here. There's also a popular French-inspired cafe attached, so you can unwind with a cup of coffee and cake while you peruse your purchases.

Check out the mini bespoke stores in the Aoyama Heights building.

5.

THE PALACE BUILDING

Palace Aoyama, 6-1-6 Minami-Aoyama, Minato-ku
Omotesando station, exit B1

Make sure you spend an afternoon floating around the beautifully curated bespoke stores that line the first floor of this '70s apartment block. **Higashi** showcases the finest examples of handmade Japanese homewares, including ceramics, teapots and cutlery. Each piece is so exquisite you'll wish you'd packed an extra suitcase. **Arts & Science** is the main store here and a number of other shops come under its banner. One of them is **At the Corner**, a stunning, dark and minimalist design shop that sells an exceptional range of experimental clothing and luxurious homewares.

Sister store **Shoes and Things** employs Japanese leather and craftsmanship to make the most immaculate footwear. On the lower level is Arts & Science's cafe, **Down the Stairs**. You might need some sustenance after browsing the fine wares in the design stores above, so head down those stairs and order a delicious organic lunch from the cafe's hearty menu. You can trial the crockery and cutlery sold in the Arts & Science stores while you're at it. Down the Stairs also sells a range of t-shirts, bags and food if you're not already completely shopped out.

TOKYO TIP
The serene Nezu Museum
has beautiful gardens and
a lovely cafe.

6.

GONBĒ

5-9-3 Minami-Aoyama,
Minato-ku
3406 5733
Open Mon–Sun 11.30am–10pm
Omotesando station, exit B1

A cobblestone pathway, kanji menus and relics of old Japan make for a beautiful entry into this simple and simply perfect Aoyama eatery. The atmosphere continues inside with dark-wood beams, screens, low-lit lamps and a small tatami section. If the quaint interior doesn't charm you, the old-world cheery service will. So will the lunch sets: delicious soba and udon noodle dishes come with a tempura, tonkatsu (pork deep-fried in breadcrumbs) or sashimi rice bowl. For ¥700 to ¥980, this is a bargain in upscale Aoyama.

7.

AOYAMA FLOWER MARKET TEA HOUSE

5-1-2 Minami-Aoyama,
Minato-ku
3400 0087
Open Mon–Sun 11am–6.30pm
Omotesando station, exit A5

As you enter this secret garden hidden behind the Aoyama Flower Market, the scent of flowers wafts overhead. Inside the beautiful teahouse, intricate lights entwine with dangling blooms, and glass-topped tables reveal vines that curl around your feet. Take a seat and choose from a wide range of specialist tea blends and herbal teas, perhaps channelling your inner quaintness with an Earl Grey accompanied by scones and cream (¥1800). Dainty little cakes are also on the menu, as is French toast, but our pick is the 'flower palfet', a muddle of rose jelly, ice-cream and mousse studded with fresh flowers. Grab a bouquet or one of the teahouse's signature scents on your way out and take some of this little patch of heaven with you.

A TO Z CAFE

5F, 5-8-3 Minami-Aoyama,
Minato-ku
5464 0281
Open Mon–Sun
11.30am–11.30pm
Omotesando station, exit B1

The centrepiece of this whimsical 5th-floor cafe is an amazing wooden house, a permanent art installation that's a reconstruction of pop artist Yoshitomo Nara's studio. Mastering the art of kawaii – that cute quality that pervades Japanese culture – Nara's paintings of impish, wide-eyed moppets line the walls elsewhere in this cafe, peering out of intimate recesses and nooks, seemingly watching you as you eat. The rest of the cafe is all painted pipes and wooden beams combined with a mashup of found furniture.

Between 11.30am and 2pm, the set lunch is a steal at ¥1000. Otherwise join the crowd of bohemian locals, art students and couples and mooch away the afternoon sipping coffee and grazing on the house speciality of pumpkin coconut cream cake. If you can't get a table near the wooden house, get one next to the window for a fantastic view over the rooftops of Aoyama. At night, the mood shifts as a DJ hits the decks and coffee moves over for cocktails.

ROPPONGI AND AZABU-JUBAN

Roppongi has long held the crown as the go-to precinct to party all night and catch the last train home. Chaotic and noisy, it has looming overpasses and streets so wide you can't see the other side. While its seedy reputation has been hard earned and is well deserved, the precinct has undergone a cultural renaissance over the last ten years with the emergence of an 'art triangle' featuring some of the world's finest galleries and architecture.

Azabu-Juban is right next door, but it's more sedate, with a village-like atmosphere, cobbled streets, traditional shops and family businesses which are in stark contrast to party-central Roppongi.

SHOP

1. Uguisu the Little Shoppe
2. Aoyama Book Center
3. National Art Center Museum Shop
4. Mamagen

EAT

5. Gogyo
6. Shiroikuro

EAT AND DRINK

7. Udon Kurosawa
8. Ukai

21 21 DESIGN SIGHT
Hinokicho Park
0 100 m
SUNTORY MUSEUM OF ART
Midtown Tower
Midtown West
Tokyo Midtown
Midtown East
FUJIFILM SQUARE
GAIEN HIGASHI
Toei Oedo Line
DORI
DORI
TO NATIONAL ART CENTER MUSEUM SHOP & GOGYO (SEE MAP LEFT)
HAIYUZA THEATRE
Mikawadai Park
ROPPONGI
ROUTE 3 SHIBUYA ROUTE
ROPPONGI
EXPRESSWAY
FamilyMart
METROPOLITAN
Tokyo Metro Namboku Line
ROPPONGI STATION
GAIEN
LAWSON
Tokyo Metro Hibiya Line
AOYAMA BOOK CENTER
FamilyMart
Post office
HIGASHI
Tokyo Metro Hibiya Line
LAWSON
DORI
Starbucks
MAMAN SCULPTURE
GAIEN
SAVOIR VIVRE & IMA GALLERY
EXPRESSWAY
Mori Tower & Art Museum
Mohri Garden
HIGASHI
Toei Oedo Line
港区 MINATO-KU
TO UKAI
METROPOLITAN
MUSEUM CONE (ENTRANCE)
TV Asahi
DORI
UGUISU THE LITTLE SHOPPE
N
TSUTAYA
International House of Japan
UDON KUROSAWA
Tokyo Metro Namboku Line
GAIEN
Toei Oedo Line
HIGASHI
FamilyMart
MOTOAZABU
AZABU-JUBAN STATION
LAWSON
MAMAGEN
SHIROIKURO
Starbucks
McDonald's
7-Eleven
Post office
TAKISHITA
AZABU-JUBAN STATION

1.

UGUISU THE LITTLE SHOPPE

Room 7, 3-3-23 Azabudai,
Minato-ku
6426 5949
www.uguisulittleshoppe.com
Open Fri–Sat 12–7pm,
Sun 12–5pm
Roppongi station, exit 2

Tucked away in a quiet lane just a ten-minute stroll from the madness of Roppongi station is a charming 1930s building housing this craft and homewares store. Owner Hiki has curated a beautiful and playful collection of must-have and hard-to-find items from Japanese and international makers. Linen, jewellery, tableware and stationery are handmade with love here, and you'll adore the contemporary takes on Japanese classics like furoshiki (wrapping cloths), candles and washi (patterned paper tape). Our top picks are Aiko Fukawa's cut-out cat stationery, Polkaros' kawaii (cute) hand-painted vases and the delicate Harvest jewellery, but there's plenty more to love. You can even keep shopping once you get home: Uguisu has an online store.

TOKYO TIP
Have a look at the
gorgeous little Gallery
Su next door to Uguisu
the Little Shoppe for
unique exhibitions.

2.

AOYAMA BOOK CENTER

6-1-20 Roppongi, Minato-ku
3479 0479
Open Mon–Sat 10am–5pm,
Sun 10am–10pm
Roppongi station, exit 3

You'll lose hours in this dapper bookstore, a welcome sanctuary from the intersections, overpasses and chain stores of Roppongi central. For non-Japanese speakers, and there seem to be a lot of them in Roppongi, there's a great selection of novels, magazines and books in English. The Japanese design, graphics and art books are the stars here though, and you don't need to be able to read them to know how good they are: just look at the pictures! Same goes for the fantastic range of Japanese art and fashion magazines. If you can't find what you were looking for here, there's a very good chance you'll find something you weren't looking for.

3.

NATIONAL ART CENTER MUSEUM SHOP

7-22-2 Roppongi, Minato-ku
5777 8600
www.nact.jp
Open Wed, Thurs and
Sat–Mon 10am–6pm,
Fri 10am–8pm
Nogizaka station, exit 6

A curvaceous architectural marvel in steel and glass, the National Art Center is a new addition to Roppongi's cultural landscape. In the unlikely event that there isn't an exhibition on that appeals to you, it's still worth making the trip here to admire the building and go shopping in one of the best museum shops on the planet. Describing the wares for sale, the website says it all: 'chaotic energy let loose by artists and designers from across the world'. Not your standard postcards of Mona Lisa or expensive catalogues then … Instead you'll find some choice items curated especially for the shop, plus a great range of art-related trinkets and everyday objects.

The National Art Center's cafe Brasserie Paul Bocuse le Musée offers a ¥1800 three-course set menu in one of Tokyo's most stunning contemporary buildings.

4.

MAMAGEN

1-8-12 Azabu-Juban, Minato-ku
3583 0962
Open Mon–Sun 10am–8pm
Azabu-Juban station, exit 1

Soybean crackers are a staple snack in Japan, but some places, like Mamagen, elevate them to an art form. To find this shop, just follow your nose down the cobblestone streets that smell of charred eel and grilled chicken and whisper of yesteryear Tokyo. Inside, colourful packs of crackers line the walls in a multitude of flavours and varieties, both sweet and savoury. If you can't work out what's in a pack, there are usually samples nearby, so you can try before you buy. The shio kaki (salted, deep-fried crackers) are insanely more-ish. Even if you're not crackers for crackers, buy them for a friend: they're considered an excellent and simple gift.

5.

GOGYO

1-4-36 Nishi-Azabu, Minato-ku
5775 5566
Open Mon–Sat 11.30am–3am,
Sun 11.30am–12am
Roppongi station, exit 1C

Gogyo is an institution in Kyoto, a ramen joint set in a stunning old building with a great story to tell. While this Roppongi branch doesn't have an interesting story or particularly spectacular surrounds, it does have the same delicious ramen (ask for the English menu). Years of experience have gone into perfecting its version of the Japanese staple, so expect perfectly cooked noodles, more-ish soup and ever-so-tender slices of pork. Our pick is the unforgettable burnt-miso ramen, a dark, rich broth with lip-burning oil floating on top. Its deep smoky flavour makes it irresistible, and it's also perfect after a late-night drinking session to soak up that one too many.

江戸
たぬき

酒と麺

6.

SHIROIKURO

2-8-1 Azabu-Juban, Minato-ku
3454 7225
Open Mon–Sun 10am–6pm
Azabu-Juban station, exit 1

Walk the quiet Azabu-Juban backstreets towards Roppongi and you'll come across this tiny local dessert store. It hasn't been around for long, but it's already carving out a name for itself as the go-to place for sweets, ice-cream and cake. A white cat will usher you in to the modern rework of an old Japanese house. Meaning 'black and white', Shiroikuro's name is fitting: many of its delicacies have a sweet white exterior that hides a dense, delicious black soybean centre. The most eye-catching dessert is probably the Swiss roll, but the popular choice is the salted mocha dumpling. Go on: see if you can eat just the one.

7.

UDON KUROSAWA

6-11-16 Roppongi, Minato-ku
3403 9638
Open Mon–Fri 11.30am–3pm & 5–11pm, Sat–Sun 11.30am–11pm
Azabu-Juban station, exit 4

This small, rustic restaurant specialises in the lighter Kyoto-style udon noodle. While all the dishes are excellent, locals come for the delicious curry nanban, an udon dish with a dashi stock. Our pick, though, is the fresh seasonal udon. Udon Kurosawa is particularly good at night, when it broadens the food menu to include izakaya classics. Ask to try delicious regional sakes, delivered in handmade ceramics. There's a rumour that this place is owned by famous film director Akira Kurosawa's son. Judging by the restaurant's attention to detail and excellent standards, we wouldn't be surprised if it's true.

TOKYO TIP
The night view from the
Mori Art Museum tower
is spectacular.

UKAI

4-4-13 Shiba-Koen, Minato-ku
3436 1028
www.ukai.co.jp
Open Mon–Sun 11am–10pm
Akabanebashi station

Under the watchful eye of Tokyo Tower you'll find this stunning tofu-specialist restaurant cocooned in a beautiful garden. Set in a Samurai-era merchant's house that contains one of Japan's oldest sake mills, Ukai is a labyrinth of 55 intimate rooms, all sparsely furnished with tatami mats. Each of the rooms overlooks lush grounds, the thatched roof of the grill hut, koi (fish) ponds and even a waterwheel. The food here is amazing: delectable, seasonal kaiseki cuisine (a traditional, multi-course Japanese meal), augmented by the impossibly fresh tofu. Weekend lunch sets cost ¥5500 to ¥6800, while dinner will set you back anywhere between ¥87,000 and ¥129,000. While Ukai might not make it onto a cheap-eats list, it will undoubtedly make it onto your list of unforgettable Tokyo dining experiences.

御誕生日
おめ
で

Hikaru Komura, also known as Hiki, is a Tokyo native, born and raised. She works as a freelance web designer/developer and runs an online store that she started with the aim of introducing special pieces from Japan to the world. She also owns and manages Uguisu the Little Shoppe (*see* p. 66). She has been working in the Roppongi/Azabu-Juban area for over eight years.

What is your favourite gallery in Roppongi/Azabu-Juban?

There are quite a few galleries and museums in this area, so it's hard to say which one is my favourite. There are always great exhibitions held at major art museums like Mori Art Museum, the National Art Center, 21_21 Design Sight and Suntory Museum of Art. Interesting exhibitions can be seen at small galleries like Gallery Su, Savoir Vivre (for art and craft) and the IMA Gallery (for photography). All of these galleries are located in Roppongi (*see* map p. 065), except for Gallery Su, which is in Azabu-Juban.

What is your favourite design shop in Roppongi/Azabu-Juban?

Toraya at Tokyo Midtown in Roppongi. It's actually a Japanese confectionery store but it also sells lovely design products. The confectionery is true art, and the packaging, beautiful presentation and interior design are all very inspiring.

Where do you like to eat in Roppongi/Azabu-Juban?

For lunch I love going to Takishita (*see* map p. 065) in Azabu-Juban for a teishoku-style (meal set) lunch with delicious grilled fish. For a quick stop for sweets, Shiroikuro (*see* p. 072) is the best for black-bean tea, salty black-bean rice cakes and ice-cream. At night I love to go to Udon Kurosawa (*see* p. 072), which does great udon noodles.

Where do you go for a quick escape from Tokyo?

A little under two hours on the Shinkansen (bullet train), Sendai is a beautiful city full of nature, history and culture. Only an hour's flight from Haneda (Tokyo's international airport), Kanazawa is also great for a quick escape. I would head straight to the fish market for a fresh sashimi donburi (rice-bowl dish), then visit traditional art and craft stores, and the 21st Century Museum of Contemporary Art.

www.uguisulittleshoppe.com

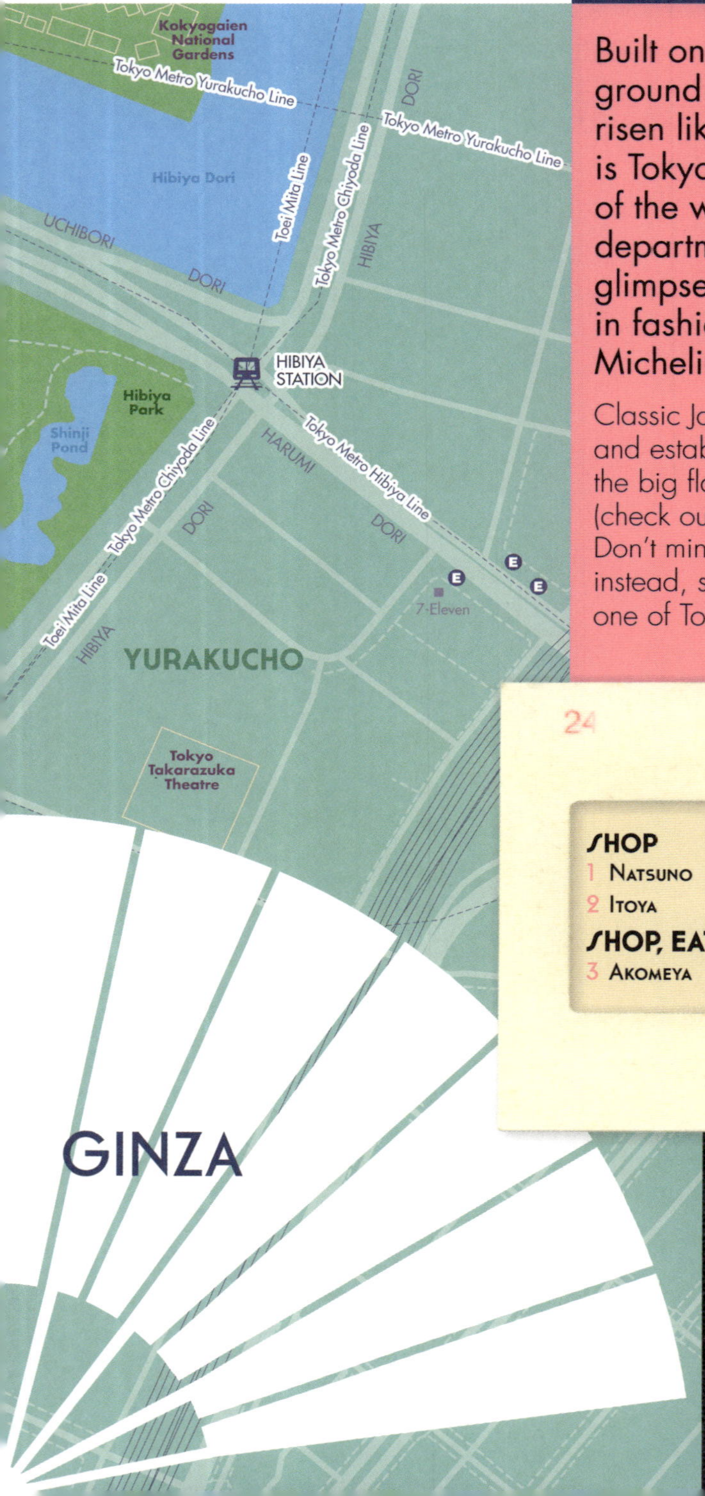

GINZA

Built on a swamp and burnt almost to the ground in 1872, this opulent precinct has risen like a phoenix from the ashes. This is Tokyo at its grandest. Home to some of the world's oldest and most luxurious department stores, it's the best place to glimpse kimono-clad women shopping in fashion boutiques and lunching in Michelin-starred restaurants.

Classic Japanese paper, fabric and incense shops, and established tempura houses, are dotted among the big flagship stores and luxe European brands (check out the eye-popping Louis Vuitton building). Don't mind the iconic Wako Clock keeping time; instead, stick around as day turns to night to see one of Tokyo's quintessential neon landscapes.

SHOP
1 Natsuno
2 Itoya

SHOP, EAT AND DRINK
3 Akomeya

EAT
4 Higashiya
5 Sushi Aoki
6 Renoir

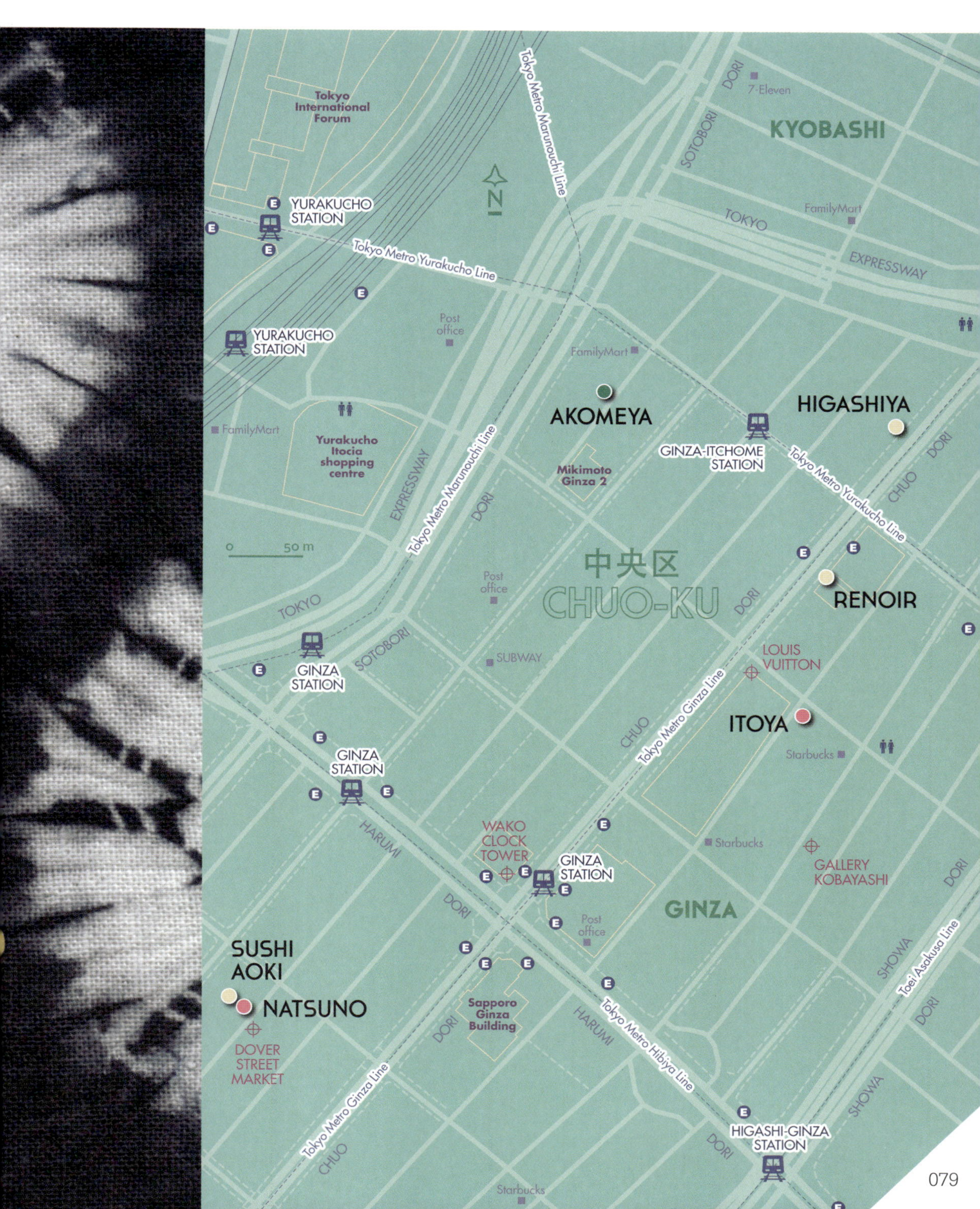

Tokyo International Forum
7-Eleven
KYOBASHI
SOTOBORI
FamilyMart
TOKYO
EXPRESSWAY
YURAKUCHO STATION
Tokyo Metro Marunouchi Line
N
Tokyo Metro Yurakucho Line
YURAKUCHO STATION
Post office
FamilyMart
AKOMEYA
HIGASHIYA
GINZA-ITCHOME STATION
Tokyo Metro Yurakucho Line
CHUO DORI
FamilyMart
Yurakucho Itocia shopping centre
Mikimoto Ginza 2
EXPRESSWAY
DORI
Tokyo Metro Marunouchi Line
中央区
CHUO-KU
DORI
RENOIR
0   50 m
TOKYO
Post office
LOUIS VUITTON
SOTOBORI
GINZA STATION
SUBWAY
CHUO
Tokyo Metro Ginza Line
ITOYA
Starbucks
GINZA STATION
Starbucks
GALLERY KOBAYASHI
HARUMI
WAKO CLOCK TOWER
GINZA STATION
GINZA
SHOWA
Toei Asakusa Line
DORI
Post office
DORI
SUSHI AOKI
NATSUNO
Sapporo Ginza Building
HARUMI
Tokyo Metro Hibiya Line
DOVER STREET MARKET
DORI
SHOWA
Tokyo Metro Ginza Line
CHUO
HIGASHI-GINZA STATION
DORI
Starbucks

NATSUNO

6-7-4 Ginza, Chuo-ku
3569 0952
Open Mon–Sat 10am–8pm,
Sun 10am–7pm
Ginza station, exit A2

The Japanese take their chopsticks seriously; it's not uncommon for them to have their own personalised set. This is where Natsuno comes in. Like an Ollivander's Wand Shop of chopsticks, there are over 2500 varieties made from bamboo, lacquer and wood, all stacked high up the walls. The colourful store also stocks hashioki, or chopstick rests, kokeshi (handmade wooden folk-art dolls) and a hotchpotch of traditional souvenirs, but it's definitely the chopsticks you're here for. Prices range from ¥300 for the simple designs right up to ¥100,000 for the serious chopstick connoisseur. Could these top-end ones have a phoenix feather or essence of unicorn in them?

TOKYO TIP
Cars are not allowed on Ginza's main streets between 12pm and 5pm on weekends, so pedestrians can amble at leisure.

2

ITOYA

3-7-1 Ginza, Chuo-ku
3561 8311
Open Mon–Sat 10am–8pm,
Sun 10am–7pm
Ginza station, exit A13

Itoya was founded in 1904 but it's definitely not stuck in its ways. Its mashup of traditional and contemporary has made it a popular destination for anyone wanting to get in on Tokyo's stationery obsession. Over six bustling floors you'll find calligraphy tools next to high-tech pens, paper products of all shapes and sizes, beautiful origami paper, fans, fabric, cards, washi (patterned paper tape) and glue, all artfully chosen. Check out its range of bags too, perfect for your iPad and laptop. The giant red paperclip sign says it all: look up to see it protruding from the building like a piece of modern art.

AKOMEYA

2-2-6 Ginza, Chuo-ku
6758 0270
Open Mon–Sun 11am–9pm
(shop); 11.30am–10pm
(cafe and bar)
Ginza station, exit A2

If you have a hankering for rice, it's safe to say that Akomeya will have what you want. It sells over 6000 items relating in some way to the great Japanese staple. Downstairs, supermarket aisles are loaded with sake, seasonings, rice desserts and more, while upstairs there's great kitchenware and utensils to eat rice with. The grain selections come from all over Japan, and you can even get your rice polished to go. In-shop cafe **Akomeya Chubo** has delicious rice-based, health-conscious dishes, while **Akomeya Bar** at the front of the store is great for a good stiff drink – a rice cocktail, perhaps?

2.

2.

2.

2.

3.

3.

HIGASHIYA

2F, Pola Ginza Building,
1-7-7 Ginza, Chuo-ku
3538 3230
Open Mon–Sun 11am–3pm &
5–9pm
Ginza station, exit A13

It'd be easy enough to walk straight past the Pola building if you didn't know what treasures lay within, but then you'd miss out on Higashiya, a luxurious teahouse. The interior is classic Japanese with a minimal contemporary makeover. Choose a bench seat or sit at a table and watch as the staff pour hot water from giant copper kettles into bowls and then whisk in green tea. Delectable lunch sets are served on equally delectable ceramics, or you can opt for afternoon tea and sweets. There are over 30 varieties of tea to try, all perfect when accompanied by delicate Japanese mochi (sweet rice cakes), which are arranged in boxes like little gems. If you're short on time, the small shop at the entrance sells Higashiya's tea, sweets and elegant homewares to take away.

TOKYO TIP
Don't miss the six floors of contemporary fashion at Dover Street Market (*see* map p. 079).

SUSHI AOKI

2F, 6-7-4 Ginza, Chuo-ku
3289 1044
www.sushiaoki.jp
Open Mon–Sun 12–2pm &
5–10pm
Ginza station, exit A2

One of the most respected (and expensive) sushi restaurants in Tokyo, Aoki prides itself on the freshest fish served at the perfect temperature. This is no sushi conveyor belt. Most people in the tiny room sit at the counter and watch the master chefs do their thing, expertly carving gleaming fish and laying it on pillows of hand-rolled sushi. Request the omakase (chef's choice) if you want one of the chefs to psychically know what you want. Our hesitation towards the sea urchin was met with a gentle coaxing – our chef knew we would like it, and we did! Did we mention that Aoki has a Michelin star? Make sure you order the lunch or dinner sets though, which you can get for ¥4200 and ¥6300 respectively. Staggering!

RENOIR

1F, 2-7-18 Ginza, Chuo-ku
3561 3856
Open Mon–Sun 8am–11pm
Ginza station, exit A13

This retro-luxe coffee-and-cake cafe is as much faded glamour as it is faded carpet. The faux '70s interior with its water features, slate pillars and green velvet chairs is so out that it's way, way in. Formerly a kissaten (classic coffee house) when Ginza glamour was at its height, Renoir is now a dandy has-been. Grab a table next to the window, order the green-tea roll cake with an iced coffee that comes with cubes of coffee jelly, sit back and relax. The older set still comes here to watch the world go by through the curved windows. You can happily light up a cigarette here too, so if you're that way inclined, make the most of it!

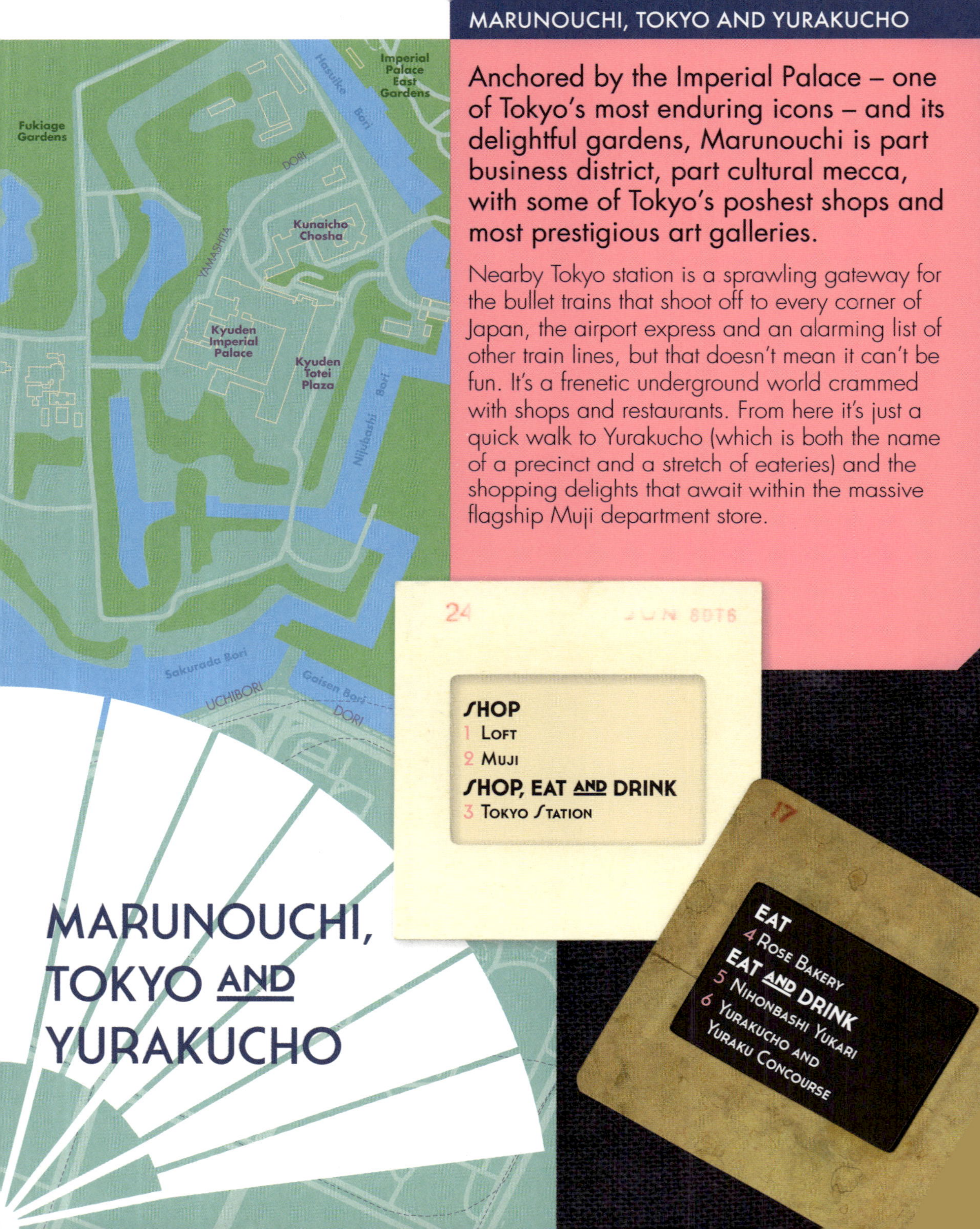

Anchored by the Imperial Palace – one of Tokyo's most enduring icons – and its delightful gardens, Marunouchi is part business district, part cultural mecca, with some of Tokyo's poshest shops and most prestigious art galleries.

Nearby Tokyo station is a sprawling gateway for the bullet trains that shoot off to every corner of Japan, the airport express and an alarming list of other train lines, but that doesn't mean it can't be fun. It's a frenetic underground world crammed with shops and restaurants. From here it's just a quick walk to Yurakucho (which is both the name of a precinct and a stretch of eateries) and the shopping delights that await within the massive flagship Muji department store.

MARUNOUCHI, TOKYO AND YURAKUCHO

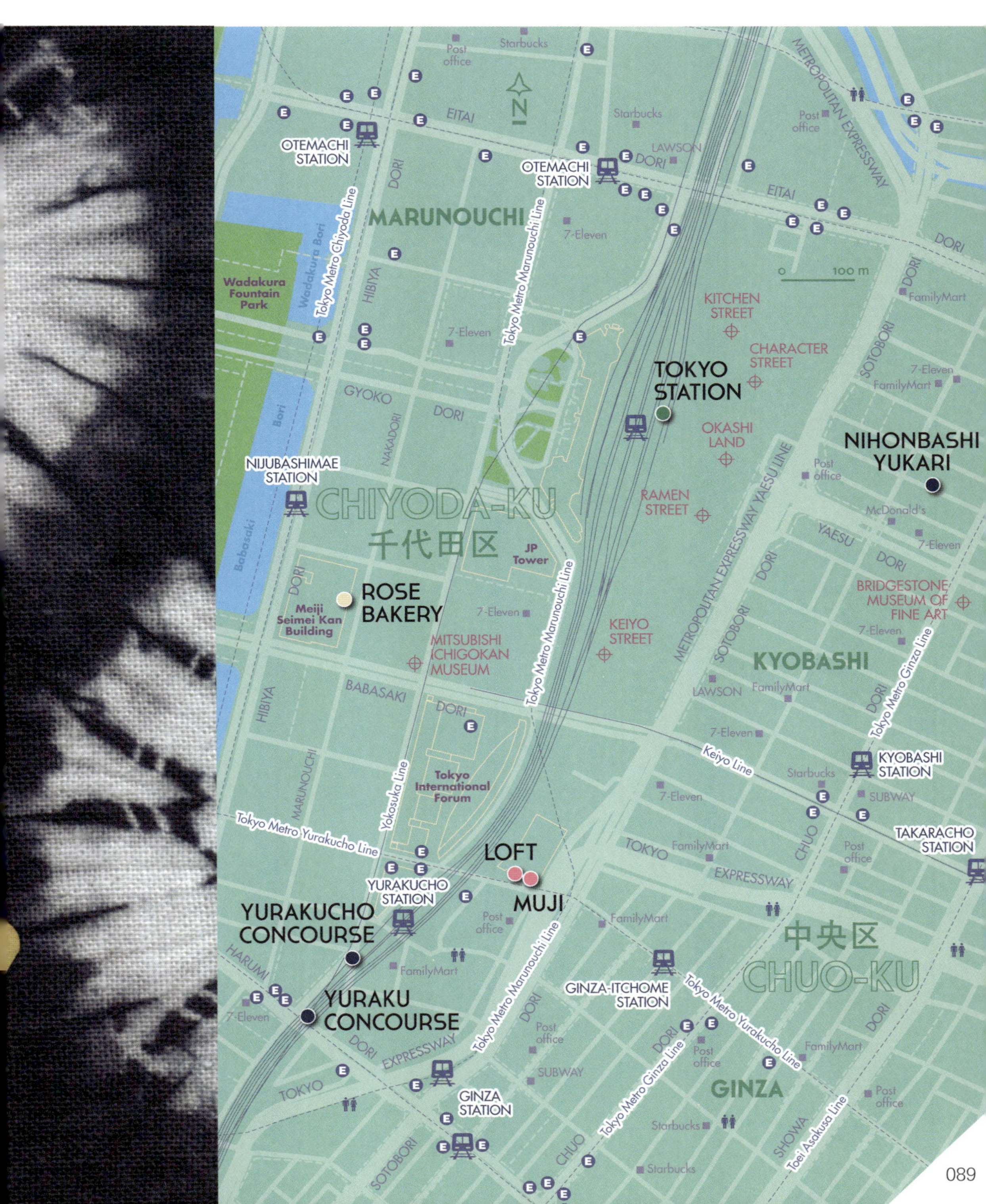

OTEMACHI STATION
OTEMACHI STATION
EITAI DORI
MARUNOUCHI
Post office
Starbucks
Starbucks
LAWSON
Post office
METROPOLITAN EXPRESSWAY
EITAI DORI
7-Eleven
DORI
Wadakura Bori
Tokyo Metro Chiyoda Line
Tokyo Metro Marunouchi Line
100 m
FamilyMart
Wadakura Fountain Park
HIBIYA
KITCHEN STREET
CHARACTER STREET
7-Eleven
FamilyMart
SOTOBORI DORI
GYOKO DORI
NAKADORI
7-Eleven
TOKYO STATION
OKASHI LAND
NIHONBASHI YUKARI
Bori
NIJUBASHIMAE STATION
RAMEN STREET
Post office
McDonald's
7-Eleven
Babasaki
CHIYODA-KU
千代田区
JP Tower
METROPOLITAN EXPRESSWAY YAESU LINE
YAESU DORI
DORI
ROSE BAKERY
Meiji Seimei Kan Building
Tokyo Metro Marunouchi Line
KEIYO STREET
BRIDGESTONE MUSEUM OF FINE ART
7-Eleven
7-Eleven
MITSUBISHI ICHIGOKAN MUSEUM
SOTOBORI DORI
KYOBASHI
BABASAKI DORI
LAWSON
FamilyMart
HIBIYA
Tokyo Metro Ginza Line
7-Eleven
Keiyo Line
KYOBASHI STATION
Tokyo International Forum
Yokosuka Line
Starbucks
SUBWAY
MARUNOUCHI
7-Eleven
CHUO DORI
TAKARACHO STATION
Tokyo Metro Yurakucho Line
LOFT
TOKYO EXPRESSWAY
FamilyMart
Post office
YURAKUCHO STATION
MUJI
YURAKUCHO CONCOURSE
Post office
FamilyMart
中央区 CHUO-KU
HARUMI
FamilyMart
GINZA-ITCHOME STATION
Tokyo Metro Yurakucho Line
7-Eleven
YURAKU CONCOURSE
Tokyo Metro Marunouchi Line
Post office
Post office
FamilyMart
DORI EXPRESSWAY
DORI
SUBWAY
Post office
GINZA
TOKYO
GINZA STATION
CHUO
Tokyo Metro Ginza Line
Starbucks
SHOWA
Post office
SOTOBORI
Toei Asakusa Line
Starbucks

LOFT

3-8-3 Marunouchi, Chiyoda-ku
5223 6210
Open Mon–Sat 10.30am–
9.30pm, Sun 10.30am–10pm
Yurakucho station, Kyobashi exit

Loft is the kind of household goods store that dreams are made of. It's a colourful selection of contemporary and functional commodities for everyday living for every room in the house. The inspired selection of homewares, stationery and lifestyle products will have you browsing for hours and mentally revamping rooms in your house for days. You'll find everything here: the latest trends in skincare and make-up, coffee pots and ceramics, brightly coloured lunch-box sets and smiley face sponges made of high-tech materials. Special celebrations and holidays are themed up: Christmas, Halloween and Valentine's Day all get the Loft makeover with catchy jingles, killer displays and other fun in-store surprises. Sharing the same building as Muji, Loft is the yin to Muji's yang.

MUJI

3-8-3 Marunouchi, Chiyoda-ku
5208 8241
www.muji.com
Open Mon–Sun 10am–9pm
Yurakucho station, Kyobashi exit

This Japanese retail giant is all about quality no-brand goods. It's everything you could want for your life, with no-fuss packaging, prices for the people and a design aesthetic that puts most other brands to shame. Sure, it's a global brand, but we're talking about the mother lode at this flagship store. Check out the 7000-plus products for sale in the lofty warehouse space set over three floors. You could come away with household goods, clothing, food, stationery and glasses to Muji up your life. There's even a Muji DIY house!

Head up to the second floor for the Muji cafe and **Muji Atelier**, a gallery showcasing Muji's creative inspirations. And if you need some extra yen (you will), there's an international ATM on the ground floor.

1.

くまモンの
とろーり☆トリュフ

1.

網戸 スッキリ!
畳 スッキリ!
壁紙 スッキリ!
【激落ち】ウェットシート
網戸用
【激落ち】ウェットシート
畳用
【激落ち】ウェットシート
壁紙用
ガラス拭き

1.

1.

2.

2.

TOKYO STATION
See map

Train stations are meant to be a way to get from A to B, but at Tokyo Station you might find yourself stuck between the letters of the alphabet. There is so much to do here you'll probably forget where you were heading in the first place, and decide to turn the station into B instead. Most of the action is at **First Avenue** at the Yaesu Underground Central exit. Here you'll find **Kitchen Street**, a labyrinth of small restaurants where some of Tokyo's culinary masters have food stalls. Nearby **Okashi Land** has excellent sweet shops where you can buy beautifully packaged gifts. There are also plenty of restaurants selling fantastic bento boxes, perfect for taking on train journeys (if you ever leave this station, that is). On **Ramen Street** you'll find eight popular ramen (noodle soup) joints, but if you don't eat meat, head east to **Keiyo Street** to find **T's Tan Tan**, which does a vegan version of ramen.

One floor down, the fun really kicks in. **Character Street** is an avenue of colourful stores, each devoted to the most beloved cartoon and anime characters. Take your kids here and they'll love you forever. Ultraman, Hello Kitty, Miffy and Moomin will all compete for your kids' attention from bold, bright and very loud stores. Many of the characters are roaming the area looking for photo opportunities.

This majestic station even has a hotel and gallery attached. 'Tip of the iceberg' comes to mind, there's so much to see and do. If you get totally lost, head straight to the station concierge!

TOKYO TIP
Grab a bento box from Tokyo Station and head to the Imperial Palace gardens for a picnic.

4

ROSE BAKERY

2-1-1 Marunouchi, Chiyoda-ku
3212 1715
Open Mon–Sun 11am–8pm
Tokyo station, Marunouchi
South exit

Clothing label Comme des Garçons did something truly wonderful when it brought Rose Bakery to its Marunouchi store. This is the land of overindulgence and upmarket shopping, but the Rose Bakery set lunch is delicious, healthy and won't break the bank. The coveted vegetable plate comes with excellent homemade bread and unsalted French butter; other mains are accompanied by rustic salads, soup and a drink. The bakery is known for its fabulous cakes, so grab one with an afternoon coffee, herbal tea or soy mocha latte. If you're heading to the Imperial Palace, order one of the takeaway lunch boxes, great for a picnic in the palace gardens. It's easy to find the bakery: just look for the spotty Comme des Garçons exterior and you'll know you've arrived.

NIHONBASHI YUKARI

Nihonbashi Yukari is owned and run by Kimio Nonaga, former champion of the Japanese television cooking show *Iron Chef*. If you think this means you're in for an expensive meal, think again. For under ¥4000 you can get the seasonal deluxe bento lunch (order in advance when you make your reservation). Ours included melt-in-the-mouth sashimi and tofu, tasting plates of grilled meats and other elegant dishes artfully arranged with delicate flower garnishes. Each small exquisite course of the bento banquet will make you feel like you're dining with the emperor, or at least Chairman Kaga (aka Shigekatsu Katsuta, host of *Iron Chef*). This is an experience you'll never forget for a price you'll barely notice.

6.

YURAKUCHO AND YURAKU CONCOURSE

4-3-3 Sotokanda, Chiyoda-ku
5298 5411
Open Mon–Sun 10am–5pm
Yurakucho station,
Central West exit

Under Yurakucho station and the rumble of passing trains you'll find Yurakucho, a 700-metre-long row of charming, old-school bars and eateries. It looks really amazing at night, as street lamps light up and roller doors reveal previously hidden yakitori and ramen joints. They're made for in-and-out drinking and dining, places where workers can grab a quick bite before heading home. One of the standout izakayas here is **Shin Hinomoto**. Pop in for dinner, then go for drinks at one of the nearby standing bars, presuming you can still stand, that is.

At the end of the Yurakucho line of bars and eateries is the Yuraku Concourse tunnel, which also has a few bars. One worth checking out is **Manpuku**, where the happy hour is so good it goes for two hours! At under ¥300 each, the drinks here are dangerously cheap and the simple bar food goes well with a night on the tiles. Peeling and faded Japanese movie posters seem to hold Yuraku Concourse together and old signs and low-lit paper lanterns recall the Tokyo of days gone by.

TOKYO TIP
Ginza and Nihonbashi are both within walking distance of Tokyo and Yurakucho train stations.

AKIHABARA

Firmly rooted in the 21st century, Akiba, as the locals call it, is a mecca for tech junkies and obsessive fans of anime and manga. It's not nicknamed 'Electric Town' for nothing: you can glimpse the future in electronics here and score the latest newfangled gadgets. If figurines, computers and vintage toys are your bag, you've hit the jackpot.

The pulsating thoroughfare of Chuo Dori is a riot of flashing lights, electronic noise, cartoon-colour buildings, toy vending machines and all-night wi-fi booths. The coffee shops here sell bottomless cups to keep you wired all day, and pastries in the shapes of anime characters are sold everywhere. Chances are, if you put on your Astro Boy outfit and go for a stroll, no-one will bat an eyelid.

LAWSON
SHOWA DORI
SAKURAINARI SHRINE
KURAMAEBASHI DORI
Tokyo Metro Hibiya Line
METROPOLITAN EXPRESSWAY NO 1 UENO
TAITO
GAME BAR A BUTTON
台東区
TAITO-KU
FamilyMart

AKIHABARA

24
JUN 8076
SHOP
1 Yellow Submarine
2 Super Potato
3 Mandarake
4 Don Quijote

17
EAT
5 Mister Donut
6 Canned Oden
DRINK
7 Game Bar a Button
8 Neko JaLaLa

KURAMAEBASHI   DORI
KURAMAEBASHI   DORI
SUEHIROCHO STATION
E
E
7-Eleven
7-Eleven
Tokyo Metro Chiyoda Line
Tokyo Metro Ginza Line
TO
GAME BAR
A BUTTON
(SEE MAP LEFT)
NEKO JALALA
Horin Park
AKIBA Place
SUBWAY
Tokyo Times Tower
Yamanote Line
Keihin-Tohoku Line
千代田区
CHIYODA-KU
CHUO
N
DON QUIJOTE
Akihabara UDX
0   50 m
MISTER DONUT
MANDARAKE
DAIDO Limited Building
FamilyMart
CANNED ODEN
CHUO   DORI
Post office
McDonald's
KANDA
MYOJIN
DORI
Akiba Culture Zone
SUPER POTATO
Akihabara Dai Building
SHOHEIBASHI   DORI
SOTOKANDA
KFC
Chuo-Sobu Line
AKIHABARA STATION
Chuo-Sobu Line
Starbucks
Tokyo Metro Ginza Line
Tohoku Jouetsu Shinkansen
SOTOBORI
DORI
CHUO   DORI
KANDA
RIVER
YELLOW SUBMARINE
Chuo Line

1.

YELLOW SUBMARINE

6F, 1-15-16 Radio Kaikan
Building, Sotokanda, Chiyoda-ku
3526 3828
Open Mon–Sun 11.30am–9pm
Akihabara station,
Electric Town exit

This is not a store for Beatles collectors as the iconic logo might suggest, but a model builder's utopia. The shop is wall-to-wall glass cases and shelves crammed with assorted kits to build tanks, ships, aeroplanes, dinosaurs, spaceships and creatures from sci-fi films. The range starts from easy-to-assemble and works its way up to way-too-many-pieces. A mostly male clientele of deadly serious modellers wanders the store with furrowed brows sizing up their next purchase. Much of the store is a museum showing detailed, ready-assembled versions of what's for sale done by known Japanese modellers. Whether you'll be able to put them together with the same skill is another thing, but it's all about the journey, right?

SUPER POTATO

3F, Kitabayashi Building,
1-11-2 Sotokanda, Chiyoda-ku
5298 5411
Open Mon–Fri 11am–8pm,
Sat–Sun 10am–8pm
Akihabara station,
Electric Town exit

Analog fans rejoice! Donkey Kong and Pac-Man are alive and well in this alternate retail universe. Super Potato is the *Back to the Future* of shopping, with three colourful floors of obsolete video games, consoles and figurines. Prices might be on the steep side, but where else are you going to get your hands on outmoded Nintendo 64, Xbox and PlayStation games all restored to perfect working order? Just when you thought the games of the not-too-distant past were gone forever, they live to be played another day! The bleeps and bloops stay with you even after you leave the store, and you'll be humming the Super Mario theme all the way home.

MANDARAKE

3-11-12 Sotokanda, Chiyoda-ku
3252 7007
www.mandarake.co.jp
Open Mon–Sun 12–8pm
Akihabara station,
Electric Town exit

Mandarake's flagship store pretty much sums up Akihabara. This ubergeek wonderland is a maze of narrow stairwells, cluttered shelves and teetering boxes, almost mimicking an Escher painting. If you're on the hunt for anime, manga, toys, creepy-cute dolls, graphic novels or figurines, then your spaceship has landed. Vintage is big here, so if you like your collectibles with a retro feel, you're sure to find that action figure or sci-fi swap card on your wish list. Warning! Warning! If you're here with junior, avoid the very graphic anime on the fourth floor, unless you want to start the birds and the bees talk early.

4.

DON QUIJOTE

4-3-3 Sotokanda, Chiyoda-ku
5298 5411
Open Mon–Sun 10am–5am
Akihabara station,
Electric Town exit

Donki, as it is affectionately known, is an out-of-control discount superstore. Look for the blue penguin mascot on Chuo Dori; he'll point the way to this retail maze of precariously balanced piles of toys, comics, homewares, alcohol and dubious pharmaceuticals. Impulse buyers won't know which way to turn. It's probably more trash than treasure, but food, gag gifts, electrical appliances, souvenirs and even luxury brand items all get the bargain treatment, and rifling through the seemingly endless stock is great fun. Be careful where you walk: turn one corner near fluffy animals and you could find yourself in an aisle full of sex toys! Note: the store is open until 5am for those times you urgently require a pair of clip-on cat ears.

TOKYO TIP

When buying electronics in Japan, remember the wattage is different from many other countries so buy a transformer.

MISTER DONUT

3-13 Sotokanda, Chiyoda-ku
3255 1655
Open Mon–Sun 8.30am–7pm
Akihabara station,
Electric Town exit

If your secret shame is a *Twin Peaks* diner-style dripolator coffee in a bottomless cup partnered with some sweet fried dough, then this is the place for you. Mister Donut has a charming old-school feel with its vintage Americana signage and interior. This being Japan though, they love to 'character up' their doughnuts. If you're lucky enough to visit during a special holiday like Halloween, your doughnut could be a ghost or a vampire. The pick of the bunch is the 'Pan de Lyon', with its adorable lion face and dough-ball mane. The green-tea-and-bitter-chocolate-filled versions are also popular buys, as are the honey churros. If you're a coffee snob or doughnut connoisseur, perhaps give this place a miss. But if you like your snacks cheap and colourful, get yourself a Misdoclub card and start earning yourself some free dough!

CANNED ODEN
Cnr Chuo Dori and Miyojin Dori,
Sotokanda, Chiyoda-ku
Open 24 hours
Akihabara station,
Electric Town exit

Akihabara is known for junk food, and Canned Oden – no, not the name of a J-pop boy band – is the ultimate Japanese fast food. So you've spent too long in Donki, it's two in the morning, and you need something special to get you through? Slot your measly ¥320 into the canned-oden machine and wrap your hands around a steaming hot tin of this traditional Japanese stew. What's not to love? It's cheap, it's in a can, and it's hot water with daikon, octopus, assorted fish cakes, cabbage, boiled eggs and a whole lot more cooked in dashi broth. Give it a go – you know you want to.

7.

GAME BAR A BUTTON

1-13-9 Taito, Taito-ku
5856 5475
Open Mon–Fri 5pm–12am,
Sat–Sun 5pm–4am
Akihabara station,
Showa Dori exit

You'll have to make like Pac-Man and chomp your way through Akihabara's streets to uncover this playful bar. A tiny brick building wedged between houses and high-rise apartments, Game Bar a Button has everything you need if you are into the combined pursuits of retro gaming and drinking. Vintage games, consoles and all manner of related equipment line the walls and benches of this bar. A mix of game fans and industry types swap stories about the good old days of video gaming as they down cold beers. A giant screen is hooked up to some retro consoles and you can plug in and play some genuine classics. It's the perfect place to toast the history of computer gaming!

8.

NEKO JALALA

1F, 3-5-5 Sotokanda, Chiyoda-ku
3258 2525
Open Mon–Fri 12–8pm,
Sat–Sun 11am–7pm
Akihabara station,
Electric Town exit

If you're missing your prized ball of fluff back home, Neko JaLaLa will give you a fast feline fix. It's a popular dating joint for locals, so popular it's probably best to reserve a spot an hour before. Then get ready for a whole world of cuteness. The cafe is home to around 16 cats, including the smoky Moco, the robust Jack and a massive beast referred to as 'the Tokyo Tower'. You can stroke them or snap pictures (without flash) to your heart's content, but just remember: no picking up! Other rules include 'don't wake up the cats' and 'don't enter drunk'. Presumably you can leave drunk though (beer is on the menu, along with tea, coffee and juices). At ¥530 per 30 minutes plus drinks, Neko JaLaLa is the cat's whiskers.

TOKYO TIP

'Maids' –
cafe staff
dressed up
in frilly white
aprons –
don't like it if
you take their
photograph.

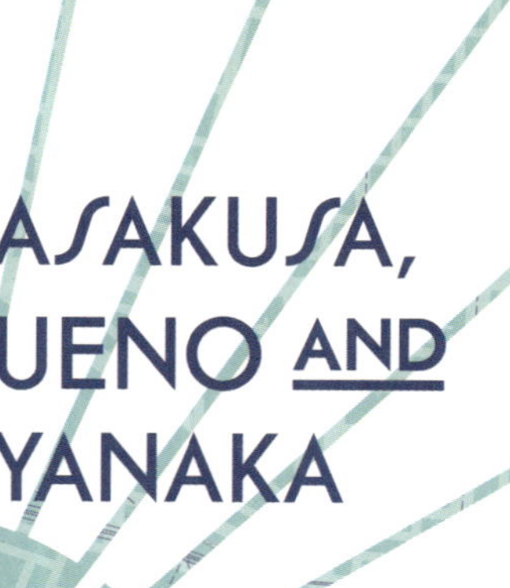

If you're after a taste of traditional Japan, head to Asakusa, whose temples and shrines give an impressive glimpse into the beauty of old Japan. It's also a tourist mecca where traditional Japanese culture meets contemporary madness.

Grab a grilled octopus tentacle on a stick and fire up your camera – photo opportunities are everywhere here, from the majestic temple Senso-ji to the towering new kid on the block, the Tokyo Skytree building. The streets and walkways are dotted with long-standing eateries, specialist snack stands and established souvenir shops. Surrounding areas Ueno and Yanaka are rich with history and have some of the finest museums, parks and traditional paper stores in the city.

SHOP
1 ISETATSU
2 BISCUIT
3 KAPPABASHI DORI

EAT
4 Asakusa Eating
EAT AND DRINK
5 Hagiso
6 Ameya-Yokocho

KOTOTOI DORI
Shotaro Ikenami Memorial Museum
TO HAGISO, ISETATSU & BISCUIT (SEE MAP LEFT)
7-Eleven
LAWSON
Post office
KAPPABASHI
NISHI-ASAKUSA
DORI
KOKUSAI DORI
Tsukuba Express
SENZOKU DORI
YADOROKU
KOTOTOI DORI
EDO-SHITAMACHI TRADITIONAL MUSEUM
Hanayashiki Amusement Park
ASAKUSA
Asakusajinja Shrine
Senso-ji Temple
DORI
Dempoin Temple
UMAMICHI
台東区
TAITO-KU
E E
7-Eleven
ASAKUSA STATION
CHINGODO SHRINE
KAPPABASHI
Higashi Honganji Temple
0   100 m
KATSUKICHI
ASAKUSA STATION
KAMINARIMON
FamilyMart
DORI
SANSADA
ASAKUSA STATION
7-Eleven
NISHIYAMA
KAPPABASHI DORI
ASAKUSA
Tokyo Metro Ginza Line
Post office
KOKUSAI DORI
KAMINARIMON
NAMIKI YABU SOBA
HATSUOGAWA
EDO
Post office
TO AMEYA-YOKOCHO (SEE MAP LEFT)
TAWARAMACHI STATION
DORI
BAZOKU
Tokyo Metro Ginza Line
ASAKUSA
DORI
ASAKUSA STATION
LAWSON
FamilyMart
E
KOMAGATA BASHI
7-Eleven
Tsukuba Express
DORI
KOTOBUKI
ACE WORLD LUGGAGE MUSEUM
Toei Asakusa Line
SUMIDA RIVER
TO TOKYO SKYTREE
KOKUSAI DORI
EDO
DORI
Toei Oedo Line   KASUGA DORI
7-Eleven
LAWSON
E

109

ISETATSU

2-18-9 Yanaka, Taito-ku
3823 1453
Open Mon–Sun 11am–7pm
Sendagi station, exit 1

Isetatsu was established in 1864 and it's still owned and run by the founding family, now in its fifth generation. It's actually two beautiful stores just a few doors away from each other, which use traditional methods to make chiyogami (wood-block-printed paper). Paper lovers will be in heaven with the stores' endless array of beautifully printed and patterned paper, kept in large wooden drawers and bought in large sheets. Themes usually relate to nature: brightly coloured flowers, leaves, seasons and fanciful tableaux of animals doing people-type things. Chiyogami used to be made into toys for children, but now it's best framed and transformed into high art. If you are looking for souvenirs, the two stores also have a range of delightful stationery, paper fans, mobiles, greeting cards and good-luck charms.

2.

BISCUIT

2-9-14 Yanaka, Taito-ku
3823 5850
www.biscuit.co.jp
Open Mon–Sun 11am–6pm
Sendagi station, exit 1

Author Masami Takewaki really knows her stuff when it comes to retro cute. She's even published a book about it, which you can buy in her excellent vintage store Biscuit. Pick up a copy and peruse the store's collection while bopping to a soundtrack of bossa nova or Japanese '60s pop. If you're looking for Japanese vintage, there's a small selection here, but it's mostly European. Retro lovers, craft fanatics and doll enthusiasts will find plenty to love. The shelves are crammed with a brightly coloured and eclectic collection of pop ephemera, including dolls in charming, detailed costumes, kewpie dolls, tins, stationery, ribbons, buttons, vintage paint sets and board games. Allow time to take in the small details that make this shop so special. We also recommend popping into Biscuit's clothing and accessories shop around the corner.

3.

KAPPABASHI DORI

Between Asakusa and Ueno
Tawaramachi station, exit 3
See map

The thoroughfare of Kappabashi Dori will literally 'cater' to your every need. Look up to see the giant chef's head with the perfectly coiffured moustache and you'll know you're entering the biggest cookware street-slash-market in the world. Tokyo has around 80,000 restaurants, and this is where their chefs shop. Leaving no stone unturned, each store has a mind-boggling array of ceramics, cutlery, crockery, utensils, chopsticks, chef uniforms, tableware and just about anything else you can think of that relates to the art, or the business, of cookery.

Make sure you check out the famous sampuru (from the English word 'sample') – the plastic display food that adorns the windows of many Japanese restaurants. Like '70s frozen moments, sampuru range from the functional to the fabulous, the comical to the disturbing – they're like little bits of pop art and make for interesting souvenirs. Now's the time to start your obsession for Japanese home cooking. At the very least you'll find some pretty things to beautify your home.

Niimi
3842-0213

TOKYO TIP
The Skyliner airport express
train goes from Ueno
to the airport, so if you
need to while away some
hours before a flight, put
your bag in a locker at
the Keisei-Ueno station
(across from the main
Ueno station).

4

ASAKUSA EATING
Asakusa station, exit A4
See map

Much of old Asakusa has remained unchanged despite the tourist influx to this area, and long-standing noodle houses, tempura joints and yakitori (grilled skewered chicken) specialists give you a chance to enjoy a taste of everyday Japanese eating from times gone by. Check out **Namiki Yabu Soba** if you want to try some authentic 'worker' soba noodles, which are slightly thicker than regular soba noodles and have a more flavoursome broth. (Note that it's closed on Thursdays.) For ramen (noodle soups), try the fresh handmade versions at **Bazoku**.

If the fried tasty goodness of tempura is your thing, do what the locals do and flock to **Sansada**, which has been around for 150 years – so it must be doing something right! Fans of deep-fried pork should hit **Katsukichi**, which has 50 different types of tonkatsu. Eel enthusiasts can get top-notch unagi at **Hatsuogawa**. Tokyo's oldest onigiri place, **Yadoroku** has perfected these popular rice triangles over its 60 years. If you need something sweeter to round off your culinary adventure, head to **Nishiyama**, which has been serving traditional Japanese sweets since the 1850s.

The Asakusa area is wall-to-wall eating, so try your luck – you really can't go wrong. If you're not sure about where to go, just join a queue!

HAGISO

3-10-25 Yanaka, Taito-ku
5832 9808
Open Mon–Sun 11am–11pm
Sendagi station, exit 1

While Hagiso still has some rustic charm from centuries ago – wooden beams and pillars of the old house it was built in remain – this is essentially new Yanaka. The cafe has been updated with clean, minimalist lines and the food is rustic-modern with only a slight nod towards traditional Japanese fare. It's a great place to while away an afternoon on your laptop with young locals. A contemporary gallery sits astride the cafe, so you can check out some challenging contemporary art while downing some booze or munching on cake and coffee. Lunch sets cost around ¥1500, and the keema curry, delicious with a fried egg plonked on top, goes down well with one of Hagiso's craft beers at night.

6.

AMEYA-YOKOCHO

Between Ueno and Okachimachi stations
Ueno station, South exit
See map

Springing up in the black market years following World War II, this narrow winding alley below the elevated train track between Ueno and Okachimachi stations is noisy, crowded and wears its old seedy charm with pride. Ameya-Yokocho is still an open-air market for locals, so make the most of it and grab something fresh to take into Ueno Park for lunch. Alternatively, slide yourself into one of the many inexpensive and delicious tempura, yakitori (grilled skewered chicken) or noodle soup joints, and sample some seafood, which the market is known for. Food carts, stand-up bars and eateries are crammed into every available niche, ensuring no real estate goes to waste. Park yourself on a bench and order beer and whatever's going; it's all good, clean, slightly seedy fun.

ホッピー
築地 活魚市場
築地 活鮮魚場
串揚げじゅうく
もつ煮
養老乃瀧
B&B
SLOT
300
200

Masami Takewaki is an author, illustrator, shop owner and avid collector of European and Japanese vintage. Since she was a student she's loved to travel and collect old things. Now she owns an antique and retro shop called Biscuit (*see* p. 111) and a clothing shop, Tsubame House, both in Yanaka.

What is so special about Asakusa/Ueno/Yanaka?

The people are really friendly and there are lots of traditional shops as well as new shops owned by unique individuals. The area also has many temples and shrines, which gives it a restful atmosphere.

What is your favourite shrine in Asakusa/Ueno/Yanaka?

Otome Inari next door to the Nezu Shrine in Yanaka is my favourite. Otome means girls, so it is a great place for girls and girls at heart.

Where do you like to drink in Asakusa/Ueno/Yanaka?

Hagiso (*see* p. 115) and Kayaba Coffee (*see* map p. 108) are my regular haunts. They are both in Yanaka in old buildings that have been renovated. Hagiso is more contemporary, while Kayaba is more of a kissaten (classic coffee house).

Where do you go for a quick escape from Tokyo?

Kyoto. There is so much to see and do there, but I go quite often just for the food. It has many different regional specialities, including sweets, bean crackers and the world-famous kaiseki cuisine (traditional multi-course dinners).

www.biscuit.co.jp

Shinjuku is a chaotic precinct of stark contrasts. Its station has 200 exits, and around 3.5 million people go through it every day, which should give you some idea of what you are in for! Sure, Shinjuku is a bit rough around the edges, but its manic nature makes it one of Tokyo's most popular destinations. Every brand, label and chain store has an outlet here, creating a seemingly endless crowd of shoppers.

It's not all madness though: some truly beautiful relics of old Tokyo butt up against the colossal superstructures. Take some time out and stroll through the peaceful gardens of Shinjuku Gyoen or head up the Metropolitan Government Building for a view that stretches to Mount Fuji.

FamilyMart
LAWSON
McDonald's
KABUKICHO
ALBATROSS G
GOLDEN GAI
7-Eleven
FamilyMart
Post office
BAR PLASTIC MODEL
Hanazono-jinja Shrine
CALICO CAT
YASUKUNI
DORI
YASUKUNI
DORI
OKADAYA
KFC
新宿区
SHINJUKU-KU
LAWSON
SHINJUKU STATION
SHINJUKU
Post office
Tokyo Metro Marunouchi Line
MEIJI
Tokyo Metro Fukutoshin Line
ISETAN
DORI
TEMPURA TSUNAHACHI
McDonald's
SHINJUKU-SANCHOME STATION
SHINJUKU
DISC UNION
Toei Shinjuku Line
SAMURAI
SHINJUKU STATION
Toei Shinjuku Line
Toei Shinjuku Line
DORI
0   50 m
SHINJUKU STATION
Tokyo Metro Fukutoshin Line
MEIJI
7-Eleven
Toei Oedo Line
FamilyMart
N
Times Square Shopping Plaza
MEIJI
Post office
TOKYU HANDS
DORI
Shinjuku Gyoen National Garden

1.

DISC UNION

3-31-4 Shinjuku, Shinjuku-ku
3352 2141
Open Mon–Sun 11am–9pm
Shinjuku station, East Central exit

For the music enthusiast, a day will not be enough in this super-sized labyrinth of CDs, DVDs and vinyl. If you can't find what you want here, you must have the most obscure taste in the world. There are seven floors in total, but the top floor is a collector's dream. Watch as people flick through racks of records before getting misty-eyed and gleefully grabbing that long-sought-after pop or rock Holy Grail. Genres jump from indie, jazz, hip-hop and punk to heavy metal, soul and disco. The test pressings lining the walls will make your jaw drop, both for their rarity and price. This is the flagship store, but Disc Union specialist music stores are dotted elsewhere around Tokyo. All worth a visit, they're tiny oddball enclaves where you'll lose hours searching for that special dub, house or death-metal find.

2.

OKADAYA

3-23-17 Shinjuku, Shinjuku-ku
3352 5411
Open Mon–Sun 10am–8.30pm
Shinjuku station, East exit

Both serious fashion designers and hobby crafters will find a lot to love in Okadaya, a rough-and-tumble haberdashery affair set over two maze-like buildings. Despite the shambolic nature of the store, the fabrics for sale here are excellent quality and the range of prints will please the most die-hard tailor. Expect the unexpected when it comes to accessories. There are floors dedicated to buttons, beads and ribbons, while elsewhere, feather boas, fancy dress, fake nails, wigs, sequins and false eyelashes will set you up for some serious showgirl glamour. It's easy to get lost in here, but that is half the fun!

ROLLING STONES
80's～ROCK
和モノレコードセール
和モノレコードセール
和モノレコードセ
来日チケット割引対象
来日チケット割引対象
来日チケ
BEATLES セール
BEATLES
BEAT
中古/USED
中古/USED
FURTHER REQU
BEAT

TOKYO TIP
Music fans can buy the 'record map' from Disc Union for ¥2200 to find out where all of Tokyo's 700 record stores are!

TOKYU HANDS

5-24-2 Times Square Building,
Sendagaya, Shinjuku-ku
5361 3111
www.tokyu-hands.co.jp
Open Mon–Sun 10am–8.30pm
Shinjuku station, new South exit

'When you visit, you find what you want', is the Tokyu Hands catchcry. Indeed, the range of homewares, stationery and travel goods here will have you wondering just when your shopping is going to stop. There's plenty here to enhance your lifestyle, but Tokyu Hands's main job is to inspire people to knit, do calligraphy, put together a sticker album or get involved in just about any kind of DIY project you can think of. The ridiculously extensive range caters for hobbyists, handy-men and -women, and professionals. If you've ever wanted to do it yourself, your journey starts here. If you haven't, don't be surprised if you come out of Tokyu Hands with a sudden passion for quilting or home renovation. While here, be sure to also check out **Yuzawaya** on the top floor of the Times Square Building, a très chic fabric and accessories store.

ISETAN

3-14-1, Shinjuku, Shinjuku-ku
3352 1111
Open Mon–Sun 10.30am–8pm
Shinjuku station, East exit

Isetan department store is
friendly, relaxed and quite
'with it' considering it's
over 100 years old. Spread
over eight buildings, you'll
find designer fashions
with eye-popping displays,
kimonos and obis (sashes)
in sumptuous fabrics, and
a generally more luxe take
on the usual department-
store fare. The real attraction
here though is the stunning
food hall, a posh basement
venue that is a mouth-
watering journey through
Japanese and international
cuisine. It definitely leans
more towards all things
French, but the perfect rows
of Japanese sweets are so
alluring you might think
you've stumbled into the
jewellery department.

5.

CALICO CAT
5F, 1-16-2 Kabukicho, Shinjuku-ku
6457 6387
Open Mon–Sun 10am–5pm
Shinjuku station, West exit

If you want some Tokyo cute overload, make sure you drop into Calico Cat. One of those only-in-Tokyo experiences, this cafe caters for the cat deprived. It's hard to spot the building, so look up to find the colourful sign, then shimmy into the two-person lift and head up to the fifth floor. Cats of all shapes, sizes, colours and breeds go about their daily business here, occasionally attended by the staff (the expression 'dogs have owners, cats have staff' has never been so appropriate). You can stroke the animals and take pictures, but there's no picking up! Enjoy coffee and cake as you admire the furry felines, but be prepared for them to spend a lot of time sleeping … as cats do.

6.
TEMPURA TSUNAHACHI
3-31-8 Shinjuku, Shinjuku-ku
3352 1012
www.tunahachi.co.jp
Open Mon–Sun
11am–10.30pm
Shinjuku station, West exit

This old-world tempura restaurant must have seen some changes since it was set up in a meandering two-storey Japanese house in 1950, but it ignores the encroaching skyscrapers and retail giants and goes about its business of providing excellent tempura to a hungry crowd. Service here is fast and friendly. Delicate crispy tempura pieces arrive with a trio of salts; the wasabi and black kombu (seaweed) salts are especially delicious. We recommend grabbing a seat at the bar and ordering the tempura à la carte to watch the chef in action; the prawn, pumpkin and aubergine tempura are all awesome. The set lunch starts at ¥1200, a seriously good deal for the crispy light tempura and a memorable delicate miso with tiny clams.

GOLDEN GAI

Shinjuku station, East exit
See map

This popular night-life district is a charming and disorderly remnant of pre-World War II Tokyo, towered over by the high-rise behemoths of modern Shinjuku. Entering Golden Gai is like being a mouse in a maze and that's not just because of the area's network of tiny alleys and lanes. It's also due to the experiments you'll be participating in as you enter each weird and wonderful drinking establishment. There are over 200 bars crammed into this unique drinking zone, so we can only give you a teensy taster of what's on offer.

For starters, there's the very cool **Albatross G**, where chandeliers, crucifixes and stuffed animal heads vibrate to some choice indie rock tunes. Also check out oddball **Bar Plastic Model** and get drunk enough to actually solve a Rubik's Cube. Then there's the downright disturbing **Tachibana Shinsatsushitsu**, where you can order medical-themed cocktails (colonic irrigation anyone?) and admire the giant silicon penis on the counter.

SAMURAI

5F, 3-35-5 Shinjuku, Shinjuku-ku
3341 0383
Open Mon–Sun 6pm–1am
Shinjuku station, South exit

You know you're in Tokyo when you get out of an elevator on the fifth floor of a nondescript building to find one of the hippest bars in the world. The first thing you'll undoubtedly notice are the thousand or so lucky cat statues. Beyond that is a room full of jazz regalia, with posters and photos lining the walls and shelves stuffed with records. Unusually for Tokyo it's quite a big space, so the whole gang can easily come along. The drinks are well priced and the vibe, helped along by a jazz soundtrack, is relaxed rather than pretentious. Be mindful of the table charge – ¥300 from 6pm to 9pm and ¥500 after nine – but really, who cares? When the drinking is this cool, everything else just fades into insignificance.

Largely unaffected by World War II bombing and the '80s construction frenzy, Koenji has the charming look and feel of pre-boom Japan. Its relaxed atmosphere hides a swirling youth undercurrent, and Koenji's late-night bars and 'live houses' (live-music venues) generate a vibrant music scene. There are also more than 70 vintage stores on Koenji's crisscross network of streets, making it a great place to spend the day trawling for retro gear.

Take a coffee break along the way: Koenji has some of Tokyo's most unique cafes. Ramen and yakitori joints crowd the streets around the station, and you'll find some of Tokyo's most creative types playing up a storm in tiny, hidden bars late at night.

100 m
FLORESTA
NATURE
DOUGHNUTS
杉並区
SUGINAMI-KU
AMLETERON
Post
office
HATTIFNATT
7-Eleven
KOENJIKITA
DIZZ
KITAKORE
BUILDING
7-Eleven
7-Eleven
CAFE
APARTMENT
CENTRAL
ROAD
McDonald's
KOENJI
STATION
Chuo Line
KFC
Chuo-Sobu Line
Chuo Line
Chuo-Sobu Line
ENBAN
LOOK
STREET
Chosenji
Temple
7-Eleven
Koenjo
Central
Park
BE-IN
RECORD
KOENJIMINAMI
7-Eleven
LAWSON
DEALERSHIP
Post
office
N

VINTAGE SHOPPING IN KOENJI

Vintage hunters beware: you'll be hyperventilating on every street corner in this pre-loved paradise. If you want to dress like Jagger, swing in '60s London gear, groove like a San Francisco hippie or put your hands in the air at a '90s rave, someone in Koenji will have your subculture covered. At last count there were over 70 vintage stores in this small precinct, with a staggering diversity. And it's not just clothes either. If you are looking for that Raggedy Ann doll to add to your collection, a classic Pyrex mug or a Beatles test pressing, we'll be surprised if you don't come up trumps.

The best way to tackle shopping in Koenji is to set a few hours aside and just wander, popping into stores as you come across them. **Look Street** and **Central Road** are good places to start. It's also worth making the trek to **Kitakore**, a bizarre, run-down mall crammed with closet-sized stores that lean towards '90s fashion. Most importantly, remember to look up, as many stores are on the second and third floors. Side streets and alleyways are also worth peering down in search of an alluring sign.

TOKYO TIP
Visit Koenji at night to catch Tokyo's up-and-coming bands.

AMLETERON

2-18-10 Koenjikita, Suginami-ku
5356 6639
Open Mon–Sun 2–8pm
Koenji station

Amleteron is Esperanto for 'love letter', which may go some way to explaining the eclectic mix of items for sale behind this store's white-cottage facade. Its welcoming interior is a haven of blonde-wood tables and shelves stocked with old books, bookmarks, fabric, paper, ceramics, postcards, letter sets, cute jewellery and even a selection of scented oils. The 'love letter' connection seems to be that all of these objects are imbued with the romance of things past. In keeping with this theme, the store also hosts vintage-letter readings performed by local writers and poets. So if you want to get in touch with your inner Jane Austen or Oscar Wilde, head on in and feel the love.

3

DEALERSHIP

2F, 3-45-18 Koenji, Suginami-ku
3314 7460
Open Mon–Sun 12–8pm
Koenji station

For collectors of American cookware and tableware, Dealership is the Holy Grail. But even if you're just a casual vintage shopper, you'll still be entranced by this museum-worthy collection. Taking up most of the space is an extensive range of Fire-King, warmly coloured, oven-safe cookware from the '50s in cheery greens, reds and blues that are so hip right now. Everything's colour-coded and beautifully arranged on the shelves, and the striped and diamond designs are the epitome of retro cool. The Americana theme also extends to advertising posters, postcards and mascots, and the Disney, Little Tikes and Charlie Brown toys will have the kids tugging at your sleeves.

SIGNBOARD ¥980
Ford
WONDER BREAD
Borden's ICE CREAM

4.

BE-IN RECORD

2F, 3-57-8 Koenji, Suginami-ku
3316 3700
Open Mon–Sun 12.30–8.30pm
Koenji station

Be-In Record is a treasure trove of collectible vinyl, a haven for the obsessive fan of first releases and test pressings. Music aficionados will have a minor meltdown here as they madly rifle through the amazing collection (Beatles and Stones fans, in particular, will be in seventh heaven). When they finally raise their heads, hours will have past, food will be needed and bored partners will be long gone. Boxes crammed with records take up most of the room; there's barely space to squeeze between them, but true music lovers won't be bothered by that. Most genres are covered, including rock, pop, punk, R&B, soul, jazz and heavy metal, and extending to psych, garage and '60s freakbeat. There's plenty of indie as well. Prices for the premium products can definitely be on the steep side, but serious collectors won't mind paying. And for music buffs with limited funds, there are still some great affordable finds amongst the impressive range.

FLORESTA NATURE DOUGHNUTS

3-34-14 Koenjikita, Suginami-ku
5356 5656
Open Mon–Sun 9am–8pm
Koenji station

Described by Floresta as the 'guilt free' or 'nature' doughnut, these tasty treats are organic and handmade in-store. If you're in the market for a doughnut though, health benefits are probably not the first thing on your mind. The animal doughnuts are the major drawcard, and people flock here to try sweet dough in the shape of panda bears, smiling cats, rabbits, frogs and tigers, to name but a few. Little details like crunchy ears sweeten the deal further. These are pretty much the cutest looking doughnuts you'll ever see, treats to make your heart melt, but not your wallet (they're only around ¥120 to ¥220 each). And, of course, they're delicious, especially with an afternoon coffee. On hot days try a granita, which comes with a tiny doughnut creature bobbing on top, so cute you won't want to eat it. No doubt your tastebuds will win out in the end, so make sure you snap some pictures first!

6.

HATTIFNATT

2-18-10 Koenjikita, Suginami-ku
6762 8122
Open Mon–Sat 12pm–12am,
Sun 12–11pm
Koenji station

Watch your head as you enter this little cafe: the door is like an entrance to a pixie house. The fairytale theme continues as you climb the narrow stairs and head into the 'tree house', a cute wooden room with stepladders that lead to tiny tatami spaces. The walls are covered with naive art, brightly coloured children's pictures that make the place look a bit like a nursery. This makes the hardcore alcohol on the menu a bit confusing, but it's the inner child they're going for here, so sit back and wrap your hands around a hot mug of 'glamour nanna' coffee and Baileys. You can also get food here, mostly pizza, pies and cake; press the buzzer to summon your waiter when you're ready to order. If you've been on the Baileys, be careful when you head back down the stairs: they're steep!

CAFE APARTMENT

2F, 3-2-15 Koenjikita,
Suginami-ku
3339 8339
Open Thurs–Tues 3–11.30pm
Koenji station

This upstairs cafe has been designed to look like a Japanese apartment. Many Tokyoites live in spaces just like this – with low furniture, throw cushions, indoor plants and vintage books – so for locals it's a home away from home and for the rest of us it's an education. Slip your shoes off, put on some cosy slippers and settle in. Try the royal mango milk tea, or, if you like to relax with something stronger when you're at home, choose something from the alcoholic drinks menu. Food-wise, there are curries, pastas and salads on offer, and desserts that change with the seasons and have an around-the-world theme. Make sure you create some timeless art on your placemat with the coloured pencils provided. And please respect your hosts' wishes: they politely ask that you don't photograph the interior of their little home. You're welcome to snap the photogenic food though!

8.

DIZZ

3-5-17 Koenjikita, Suginami-ku
3336 2545
Open Mon–Fri 5pm–1am,
Sat–Sun 4pm–1am
Koenji station

Dizz is a warm, friendly izakaya set in a charming early-20th-century building on Koenji's Central Road. Paper lanterns swing outside and the character continues into the building where vintage Japanese posters seem to keep the walls glued together and kanji menus dangle over a bustling bar. There are many small dishes on offer and the usual extensive izakaya drinks list, but the tasty grilled meat and vegetable skewers are the real star here, especially the chicken with shiso (a type of mint) leaves. Stuffing your face will only set you back ¥2500 or so. Dizz is a great place to eat like a local, and the young Koenjiites tending the bar make it a lively spot to see the precinct in action at night.

やきとり
串焼き処 ディズ
やきとり
国産朝締め鶏の看板炙焼
みそダレ焼
名物!!煮込み
ホッピー
HOPPY
サッポロラガー

A former radio producer and DJ from Melbourne, Australia, Kim Jirik is currently a resident of Tokyo. When not exploring the city's local music communities, he can be found partaking in national pastimes involving food, booze and karaoke.

What do you like about living in Koenji?

I first visited Koenji because it is known for its live-music venues. Then I found out that there were all these great places to eat, as well as many second-hand stores. I'm always struck by the great energy in Koenji, helped along by the punk rockers, young immigrants and families who call it home.

What is your favourite live-music bar in Koenji?

Visiting a 'live house' (live-music venue) can be more about the experience than the music, so I'm often happy to take a punt. My go-to live house is Enban (*see* map p. 131). It's a record store dedicated to avant-garde local music during the day and a live house after dark. Check its schedule; it occasionally hosts non-musical events too.

Where do you like to eat and drink in Koenji?

Koenji is full of great yakitori (grilled skewered chicken) restaurants that spill out onto the street. For something special, I head to Dizz (*see* p. 140) for yakitori – you pay a little more per skewer, but they're unbeatable. If you go, you have to try its chicken skewers with shiso (a type of mint) leaves or the wasabi infused with yuzu (a citrus fruit).

Where do you go for a quick escape from Tokyo?

I head for the hills. Koenji is on the Chuo line, which ends up in Nagano prefecture. I seem to find myself there a lot. I recommend visiting Narai in the Kiso Valley. It's a beautiful old village at the historical halfway point between Kyoto and Tokyo.

Perched on the edge of Inokashira Park, this residential neighbourhood has a very local feel. It's the perfect antidote to the madness of the big city and only 20 minutes from Shibuya by express train. You can choose your own adventure here: ride a bicycle down Nakamichi Dori to check out the independent handmade stores. Have dinner and drinks in the tiny bars and eateries of Harmonica Yokocho. Stroll down the covered lanes of the Sun Road Arcade.

A picnic in Inokashira Park in cherry blossom season makes for the perfect day. Cruise the park's lake in the swan boats or stop off at the Ghibli Museum, a mecca for animation fans.

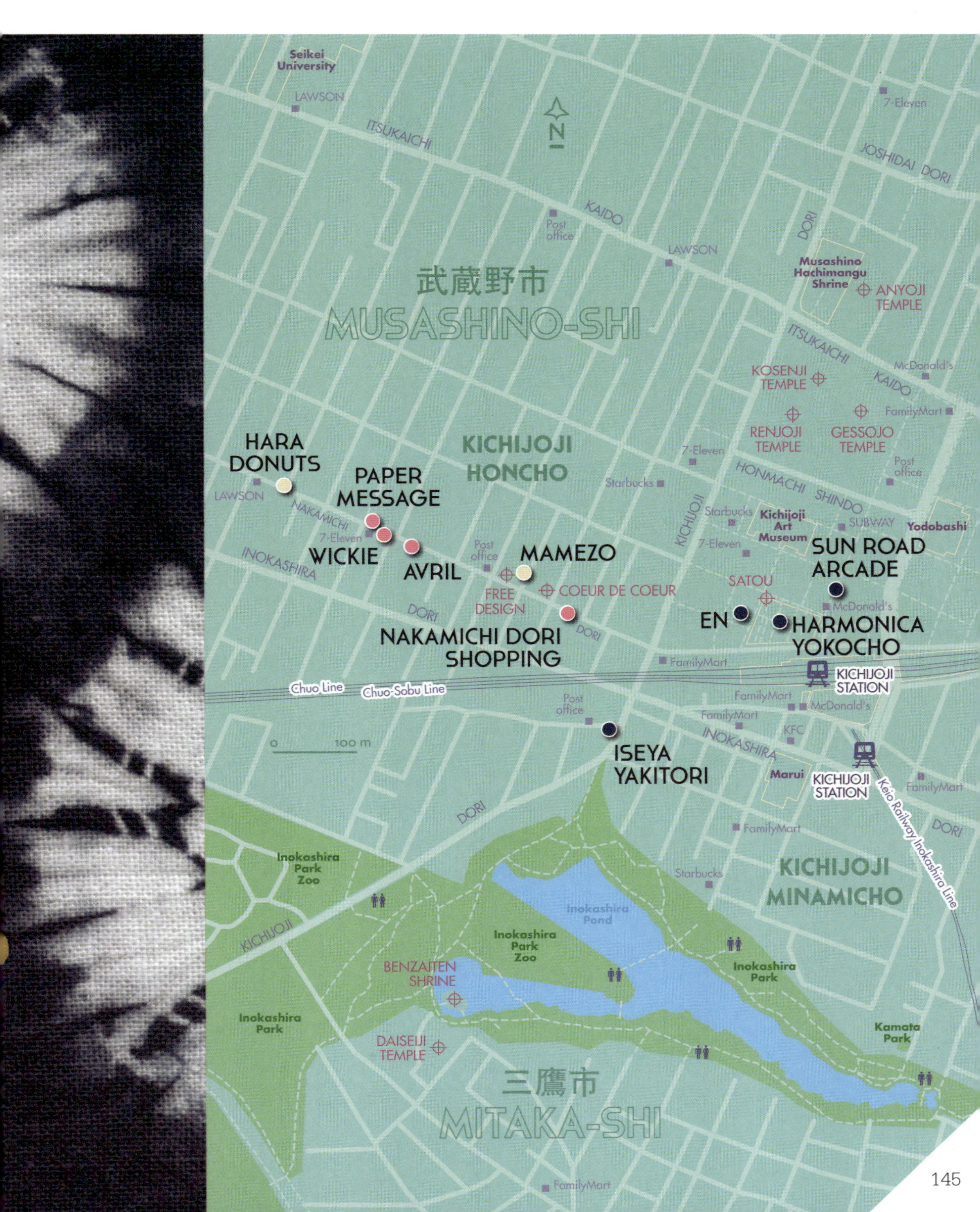

Seikei University
LAWSON
ITSUKAICHI
KAIDO
Post office
LAWSON
7-Eleven
JOSHIDAI DORI
DORI
Musashino Hachimangu Shrine
ANYOJI TEMPLE
ITSUKAICHI
KAIDO
武蔵野市
MUSASHINO-SHI
KOSENJI TEMPLE
McDonald's
KICHIJOJI HONCHO
RENJOJI TEMPLE
GESSOJO TEMPLE
FamilyMart
Post office
HARA DONUTS
Starbucks
7-Eleven
HONMACHI SHINDO
LAWSON
PAPER MESSAGE
NAKAMICHI
7-Eleven
Starbucks
KICHIJOJI
Kichijoji Art Museum
SUBWAY
Yodobashi
WICKIE
INOKASHIRA
AVRIL
Post office
MAMEZO
7-Eleven
SUN ROAD ARCADE
FREE DESIGN
COEUR DE COEUR
SATOU
McDonald's
EN
HARMONICA YOKOCHO
NAKAMICHI DORI SHOPPING
DORI
DORI
FamilyMart
KICHIJOJI STATION
Chuo Line
Chuo-Sobu Line
FamilyMart
FamilyMart
McDonald's
Post office
INOKASHIRA
KFC
0   100 m
KICHIJOJI STATION
ISEYA YAKITORI
Marui
Keio Railway Inokashira Line
FamilyMart
DORI
DORI
FamilyMart
KICHIJOJI MINAMICHO
Inokashira Park Zoo
Starbucks
KICHIJOJI
Inokashira Pond
Inokashira Park Zoo
Inokashira Park
BENZAITEN SHRINE
Inokashira Park
Kamata Park
Inokashira Park
DAISEIJI TEMPLE
三鷹市
MITAKA-SHI
FamilyMart

NAKAMICHI DORI SHOPPING

Nakamichi Dori is great for a Sunday stroll … especially if you're into shopping. Creative handcraft stores, inspired fashion designers and dedicated vintage collectors make it one of Kichijoji's prime destinations. We've already singled out a few of our favourites on this street – Wickie (*see* right), Paper Message (*see* p. 148), Avril (*see* p. 149) and Hara Donuts (*see* p. 150) – but there's plenty more to get excited about.

If you're looking to send parcels or letters, head to **Pack Mart**, an old-fashioned stationery store brimming with postage bags, tapes and things that tie, wrap and bundle. The charming blue-striped exterior of **Coeur de Coeur** will draw you into this shop that sells cute stationery and new and vintage homewares. **Poool** makes chic women's wear, beautiful linen pieces in timeless designs. Up a steep flight of stairs is **Free Design**, a small space crammed with international and local homewares and novelties. And that's just the tip of the iceberg. It pays to take your time and really savour this street; you never know what you'll uncover.

WICKIE

3-2-9 Kichijoji Honcho, Musashino-shi
0422 268 792
Open Mon–Fri 12–8pm, Sat–Sun 11am–8pm
Kichijoji station, North exit

We always look forward to visiting Wickie on a stroll down Nakamichi Dori. The owner's well-curated mixture of beautiful new and mid-20th-century objects from Japan and the world is always good for a browse. Scandinavian mid-century is well represented with ceramics by Arabia and Rörstrand, amongst many others. Elsewhere there's quite a rustic feel to the collection. You can pick up beautiful linen coasters and tiny soy bottles for around ¥500 to ¥1000 and they'll be some of the nicest things you'll ever own. The store also has great retro signs, vintage Chemex (a type of pour-over coffee maker) and American ephemera. Newer items include tea towels, handkerchiefs, tiny wooden spoons and even a small range of shoes and clothing that won't break the bank. Well stocked and a beautiful stop on any Kichijoji amble.

1.

1.

1.

2.

2.

2.

PAPER MESSAGE

4-1-3 Kichijoji Honcho,
Musashino-shi
0422 271 854
Open Mon–Sun 11am–7pm
Kichijoji station, North exit

The art of communication is alive and well in Kichijoji and if you want to send a letter, or just slip someone a note, Paper Message will help pretty up your correspondence. Stationery nerds, lovers of DIY crafts and hobbyists will find much to adore in this hands-on paper store. Just so you know, the staff here have OSD (obsessive stationery disorder), and most days you'll find them drawing their own characters, folding envelopes, making up stamps and working out new and beautiful ways to send cute-as-a-button messages to that special someone. The shop itself is a riot of colour; bright illustrations line the walls and pop out from writing paper, origami, ribbons and brooches. You're sure to be inspired to set aside email occasionally and find new and inventive ways to go old school with your correspondence.

AVRIL

2-34-10 Kichijoji Honcho,
Musashino-shi
0422 227 752
Open Mon–Sun 10am–7pm
Kichijoji station, North exit

- -

This yarn store is a must-visit for anyone into knitting. Different wools are sold by the weight here, and you can pick them from the brightly coloured array of cones that line the walls in the main room, or from the more outrageous fleeces kept in a room out the back. If you're feeling especially crafty, combine the different colours, gauges, textures and styles to personalise your yarn. Make sure you check out the great selection of knitting tools, needles and materials too, and pop into the side room where locals meet and knit their own eclectic blends of wool into jumpers, scarves, baby booties and whatever else takes their fancy.

5.

HARA DONUTS

4-13-15 Kichijoji Honcho,
Musashino-shi
0422 220 821
Open Mon–Sun 10am–7pm
Kichijoji station, North exit

You'll have to head to the end of Nakamichi Dori to find the stylishly rustic white frontage of Hara Donuts, but it's well worth the trip. A Hara doughnut is not exactly guilt-free, but compared to a regular doughnut it sure is. Made from tofu pulp rather than dough, these small but perfectly formed rings are described by the shop as 'the way mum used to make them', although if anyone had a mum who made doughnuts like this, lucky them. There are more than 80 flavours, but we still managed to find a favourite (the white chocolate), and at less than ¥200 each they're a bargain. They are also nuggety little treats that will fit the bill for any doughnut craving and may even put you on the path to righteousness.

MAMEZO

2-18-15 Kichijoji Honcho,
Musashino-shi
0422 217 901
Open Mon–Sun 11am–10pm
Kichijoji station, North exit

The Japanese have their own unique take on curry and Mamezo has perfected a subtle yet more-ish variety that will definitely have you going back for more. This well-known curry house has been in Kichijoji since the '70s and still has a bit of a hippie vibe going on. Wooden beams and white stucco walls, clay figurines and oddball pictures lend an eclectic feel to the interior. It's small, but if you have to wait for a seat it's worth it. The menu of classic curries (available in English) ranges from beef and chicken to different types of vegetables. At ¥850 to ¥1000 with a coffee or juice, each dish is a real bargain. Our favourite is the yasai (vegetable) curry, a rich delicious sauce ladled over rice with mini okra, tiny tomatoes that pop in your mouth and a side dish of pickles. Order it with boiled tamago (egg) on top for bonus flavour. Don't forget to grab some of Mamezo's take-home sauce on the way out.

EN

2F, Masakae Building, 1-2-8,
Kichijoji, Hon-cho, Musashino-shi
0422 290 309
Open Mon–Fri 11.30am–3pm
& 5pm–12am, Sat–Sun
11.30am–12am
Kichijoji station, North exit

En is hidden away on the second floor of a glorious historic house on Harmonica Yokocho's edge. Head up the stairs, put your shoes in a locker and glide into this tranquil haven, with its interior of tatami mats, low tables, shoji screens and beautiful cushions. Lunchtime is when you'll get the best value; there are ten different lunch sets (and English menus available), with choices ranging from tempura and sashimi to pork cutlets and other tasty meat and fish dishes. All set lunches come with an array of small dishes that might include pickles, tofu, salad or vegetables. Prices range from ¥1280 to ¥2350 for the chef's selection, which comes with coffee or tea and a delicious genmaicha (green tea with roasted brown rice) ice-cream to finish. Wash it all down with some sake and enjoy feeling worlds away from the bustling Sun Road Arcade.

ISEYA YAKITORI

1-2-1 Gotenyama, Musashino-shi
0422 471 008
Open Mon & Wed–Sun
12–10pm
Kichijoji station, Park exit

Nearly 100 years old, this yakitori (grilled skewered meat) joint, housed in a beautiful old building on the way to Inokashira Park, is the real deal. Its old-world frontage and smoke billowing from the chimney make it easy to spot. Join the locals outside and grab some skewers and a beer at the standing bar, or head inside with students and salarymen on a budget to shared tables or tatami rooms. The skewers are mostly pork and cost a meagre ¥80 each. The lunch set is also cheap and cheerful (between ¥1200 and ¥1800). Be sure to also try the huge shumai (chunky pork dumpling), especially good when washed down with a cold beer. Most importantly, sit back and relax as the kitchen chars another round of pork skewers. Downstairs gets pretty smoky, so if you like your air a bit cleaner, it's probably best to opt for the upstairs room.

SUN ROAD ARCADE AND HARMONICA YOKOCHO

Kichijoji station, North exit
See map

If you head straight out of the north exit of Kichijoji station you'll find yourself walking the Sun Road, a covered arcade of concentrated local shopping. Its stores are mostly open to the street, giving it a vibrant market atmosphere. Meat shop **Satou** sells grilled minced meat covered in breadcrumbs. This snack is hugely popular with locals and visitors alike and the shop's ever-present queue winds past the nearby clothes and shoe shops, opticians, pharmacists and restaurants. Diagonally opposite Sato there's a fantastic **pickle shop**, where you can marvel at the selection of things that are able to be pickled, fermented and preserved, in both the recognisable and the 'what the heck is that?' categories. The **teashop** a bit further down is also excellent, selling quality Japanese teas by the bag.

If you're still feeling peckish after your Sato snack, visit the **taiyaki shop** for a fish pastry. No, these aren't pastries that taste like fish, but bream- or carp-shaped pastries filled with red-bean paste, chestnuts and custard or the more disturbing chocolate and purple sweet potato. Don't miss Harmonica Yokocho, located to the left of the Sun Road Arcade's entrance. This small rabbit warren of restaurants and bars harks back to Tokyo's past, and is a great place to visit at night. Squeeze yourself into a tiny bar here or soak up the atmosphere of bygone Japan in a specialist eatery.

TOKYO TIP
Tickets for the Ghibli
Museum must be bought
at Lawson convenience
stores, which are located
all over Tokyo. Pick your
time to visit the museum, as
you're only allowed in at
two-hour intervals.

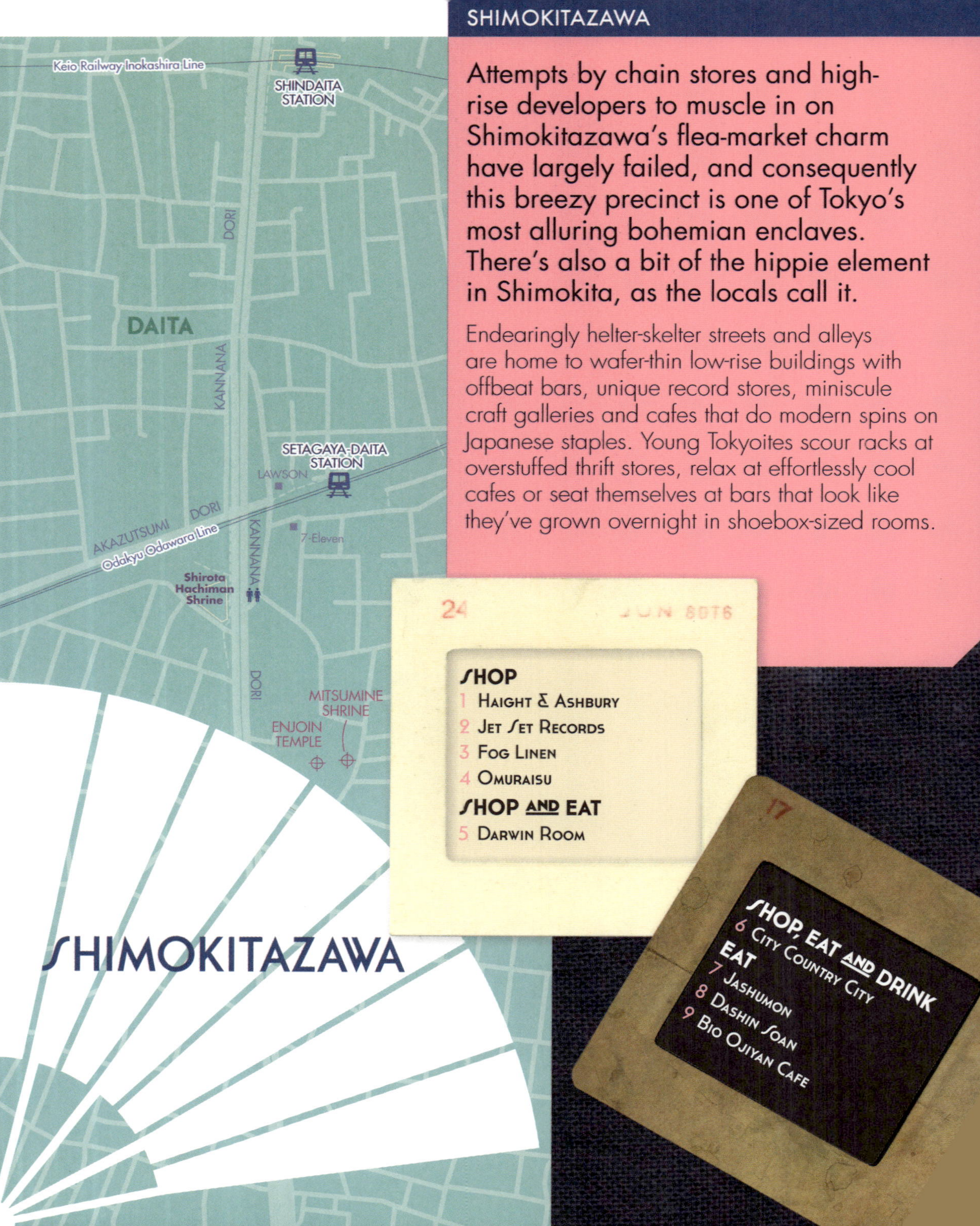

Attempts by chain stores and high-rise developers to muscle in on Shimokitazawa's flea-market charm have largely failed, and consequently this breezy precinct is one of Tokyo's most alluring bohemian enclaves. There's also a bit of the hippie element in Shimokita, as the locals call it.

Endearingly helter-skelter streets and alleys are home to wafer-thin low-rise buildings with offbeat bars, unique record stores, miniscule craft galleries and cafes that do modern spins on Japanese staples. Young Tokyoites scour racks at overstuffed thrift stores, relax at effortlessly cool cafes or seat themselves at bars that look like they've grown overnight in shoebox-sized rooms.

LAWSON
LAWSON
Post office
HAIGHT & ASHBURY
JET SET RECORDS
Odakyu Odawara line
KITAZAWA
Starbucks
LAWSON
7-Eleven
7-Eleven
FamilyMart
Keio Railway Inokashira Line
BIO OJIYAN CAFE
LAWSON
SHIMOKITAZAWA STATION
LAWSON
FamilyMart
Keio Railway Inokashira Line
FamilyMart
7-Eleven
McDonald's
FOG LINEN
CITY COUNTRY CITY
IKENOUE STATION
7-Eleven
Odakyu Odawara Line
Post office
DARWIN ROOM
DAIZAWA
FamilyMart
OMURAISU
Post office
7-Eleven
DAITA
N
Shinganji Temple
Kitazawa Hachiman Shrine
LAWSON
DASHIN SOAN
世田谷区
SETAGAYA-KU
0   100 m
7-Eleven
DORI
7-Eleven
JASHUMON
AWASHIMA

1.

HAIGHT & ASHBURY

2-37-2 Kitazawa, Setagaya-ku
5453 4690
Open Mon–Sun 12–10pm
Shimokitazawa station, South exit

Vintage-clothes shopping is a sport in Shimokitazawa and there's no shortage of stores catering to the fanatical retro hunter. A case in point is Haight & Ashbury, a rabbit warren of a store that's been perfecting its item hunting for 20 years. As the San Francisco–inspired, flower-power name suggests, there are a lot of '60s summery florals and cult lace dresses for sale here, but last-century European styles are also well represented, as are other Americana clothes. Look for the big red shoe outside and head on in; you won't be wading through flea-bitten cast-offs here. This is a tasteful selection hand-picked by people who love their job and all things yesteryear.

JET SET RECORDS

2-33-12 Kitazawa, Setagaya-ku
5452 2262
www.jetsetrecords.net
Open Mon–Sun 2–10pm
Shimokitazawa station,
South exit

Hidden away in a nondescript building, this record store is a mecca for house and techno DJs, as well as a regular shopping haunt for anyone obsessed with independent music. The collection is crammed into every nook and cranny, only leaving room for a listening station with a couple of turntables where you can try before you buy. For the claustrophobic, there's a very comprehensive online store, but you don't want to miss the atmosphere here, which harks back to the good ol' days of hunting through your favourite store for the latest vinyl releases. So have a scout around; you're sure to find something interesting, challenging or even life-changing amongst the impressive selection.

FOG LINEN

5-35-1 Daita, Setagaya-ku
5432 5610
www.foglinenwork.com
Open Mon–Fri 12–6pm
Shimokitazawa station, West exit

The philosophy at Fog Linen is simple: owner Yumiko Sekine believes in creating and selling divine products for daily use. Ten years in the making, this stylish minimalist store converts linen sourced from Lithuania into beautiful and covetable tea towels, bedding, coasters, cushions and a range of dresses and aprons. All items come in simple and tasteful earth tones, or the store's signature checks and stripes. You'll find well-heeled Shimokitazawa residents shopping here, looking for ways to add a touch of class to their homes. Make sure you plan your visit to Fog Linen: it's closed on weekends, which is almost unheard of in Tokyo.

fog
open 12:00—18:00

OMURAISU

5-29-9 Kitazawa, Setagaya-ku
3411 5262
Open Mon–Sun 12.30–7pm
Shimokitazawa station, South exit

Omuraisu is a tiny hidden gem in a Shimokita backstreet. Owner Shuichi Suma has been working on his eclectic stash of toy treasures since 1988 and it shows. Most of the store's scant real estate is taken up with cabinets crammed with brightly coloured tin toys, robots, spaceships and kokeshi (wooden folk-art dolls). Lovers of Japanese superheroes will be overawed by the selection of Astro Boy and Gigantor merchandise, and fascinated by the charming array of heroes that time forgot. The expert or novice collector will find many delights and surprises amongst the cute, vibrant and whacky inhabitants of Omuraisu.

DARWIN ROOM

5-31-8 Daizawa, Setagaya-ku
6805 2638
Open Mon–Fri 12–8pm,
Sat–Sun 12–10pm
Shimokitazawa station, South exit

Join Darwin on his voyage of evolutionary discovery at this quirky cafe with an impressively verdant exterior. Victorian-era science paraphernalia and antiquities stuff the shelves inside, and the eyes of hapless taxidermy victims follow you around the room. A self-proclaimed 'Liberal Arts Lab', the Darwin Room has the feel of a museum or library where scientists of bygone days scribbled detailed drawings of moths or orchids. Mind-bending science books are for sale, as are curios like ore samples and pendants with insects set in acrylic. Enjoy tea or coffee with cake while you consider buying a replica skull of Peking Man.

6.

CITY COUNTRY CITY

4F, 2-12-13 Shimokitazawa,
Setagaya-ku
3410 6080
Open Mon–Tues & Thurs–Fri
12pm–1am, Sat–Sun
11am–1am
Shimokitazawa station,
South exit

Seek out the tiny street
sign and take the wobbly
lift up four floors to emerge
into this pocket-sized cafe
and vintage-vinyl store.
Owner Keiichi Sokabe was
the lead singer of Japanese
'90s cult indie band Sunny
Day Service, and his love
of music shines through in
the selection of pre-loved
world music, disco, indie-
rock, house and space-funk
records for sale. Photos of
DJs and band autographs on
the wall hint that there are
good finds here, and Sokabe
makes regular international
trips to forage for quality
records. Sip a latte or a cold
beer while enjoying the tunes,
or come for the simple and
tasty pasta lunch (a very
cheap ¥1000 with tea, coffee
or juice usually included). City
Country City morphs into a
cool bar after dark.

JASHUMON

1-31-1 Daita, Setagaya-ku
3410 7858
Open Mon–Sun from 9am
(closing time varies)
Shimokitazawa station,
South exit

This cafe in a quiet, out-of-the-way part of Shimokitazawa has such an oddball charm it was used in the anime feature *Kyoukai no Kanata*. The owner, who also doubles as a magician, has amassed a fascinating and quirky collection of vintage cameras, clocks, hanging lights, guns, crosses and religious chairs. Walls are covered with photographs of popular film and music stars from the '50s who gaze down upon a classic HMV gramophone and a retro jukebox. Coffee with sugared ice cubes and a ¥650 rice-ball lunch set add extra charm. The cafe usually closes sometime after 4pm, essentially whenever the laid-back owner feels like it.

8.

DASHIN SOAN

3-7-14 Daizawa, Setagaya-ku
5431 0141
Open Mon–Fri 11.30am–3pm
& 5.30–9.30pm, Sat–Sun
11.30am–9.30pm
Shimokitazawa station,
South exit

We'll resist the urge to say 'dash in' to this soba-noodle restaurant, but definitely make it one of your Shimokitazawa must-dos. It's a bit of a hike from the station, but hey, Tokyo is not a place to stick to the main roads. Dashin Soan's charming traditional entry reveals a restaurant that raises the national noodle to an art form. Get stuck into some classic chilled soba with dipping sauce or chewy soba in a hot broth. Our pick is the duck soba, tender slices of duck in a steaming golden soup. As with all good soba restaurants, staff will bring you the cooking water to drink, a cloudy, nourishing broth that will be unlike anything you've had before.

9.

BIO OJIYAN CAFE

5-35-25 Shimokitazawa,
Setagaya-ku
5486 6997
Open Mon–Sun
11.30am–11pm
Shimokitazawa station,
West exit

This local and cosy Shimokita cafe specialises in ojiya, a congee-like savoury rice porridge that's the closest thing you'll get to Japanese comfort food. It's also one of the most versatile dishes you'll come across – it goes well with toast soldiers and egg, and meat, fish or vegetables, plus it's great for breakfast, lunch or dinner. The nori (seaweed) and sugar-dusted toast might seem unusual accompaniments, but any doubts will soon be assuaged as you dig into a bowl of this heavenly stodge. Pair it with an iced coffee in summer or a steaming matcha (green tea) latte in winter. The student, artist and vintage-kid clientele here makes for an interesting scene.

Weekend vintage shopping and people-watching in Shimokita is a Tokyo must!

Shoko Seko was born in Wakayama prefecture but has been in Tokyo for five years. She works as a toy sculptor and also sells vintage Japanese toys. She collects toys and old books and magazines, and loves to see movies, anime and art, and listen to music. She's fanatical about toys (in case you couldn't guess) and cats.

What do you like about living in Shimokitazawa?

It's a very vibrant area with a strong tradition and culture. It has many elements of old Tokyo, but is now also a hot spot for young people. It can get very crowded, but it is very safe and the backstreets are leafy. It's full of young musicians and actors and there are many 'live houses' (live-music venues) and small theatres. I work from home, but I like to get out; it feels good just walking around the place.

What is your favourite vintage toyshop in Shimokita?

Omuraisu (*see* p. 162). I always take my friends from out of town or other countries to this shop. It's full of toys from the Showa era (1926–89). The owner is very kind and has great taste. It's a very special and precious place for me.

Where do you like to eat and drink in Shimokita?

For a cup of coffee, I recommend Jashumon (*see* p. 165), a 15-minute walk from Shimokitazawa station. It has 50 years of history, and many writers and artists visit. The owner is an interesting person; he is also a magician and a collector, and you can see his wonderful antique collection at the cafe. If you visit, you must try the anmitsu coffee (coffee with agar jelly).

Where do you go for a quick escape from Tokyo?

I love to visit Kyoto. It has many of my favourite stores and temples, including Sanjusangen-do, where you can see beautiful Buddha sculptures. Osaka is not so far from Kyoto and it has its own culture. It's very noisy and the people are very friendly.

www.milbeetoy.com

Ebisu is a precinct divided. It's a shopping and business district by day, but the real Ebisu gets out of bed at 3pm, pulls on its jeans and opens a beer before heading out for an all-night party. Come evening, roller doors unveil tiny bars, eateries and night cafes that get crowded and loud very quickly.

Around the station the streets are crammed with izakayas and small stores selling handmade and boutique wares. The beer is good, of course, as Ebisu is the home of Yebisu beer, one of the world's best. Then there's Evisu jeans, also originating here and the perfect metaphor for this quirky, inventive and laid-back corner of Tokyo.

SHOP

1 Duffle with Kapital
2 Allegory Home Tools
3 Wildlife Tailor
4 Cocca

EAT

5 Afuri Ramen
6 Hinone Mizunone

EAT AND DRINK

7 Pile Cafe
8 Sakanaya Ebisu-an

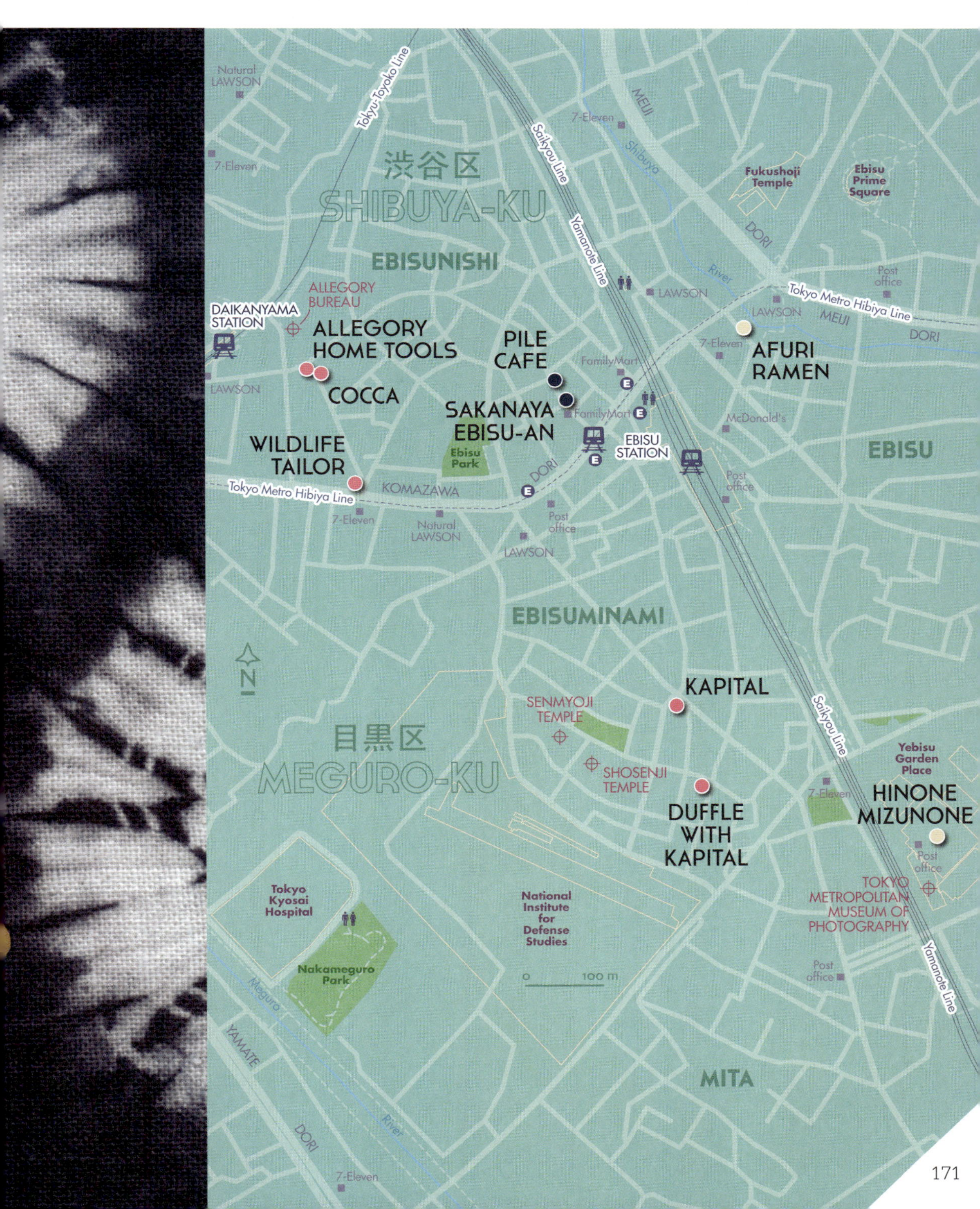

Natural LAWSON
7-Eleven
7-Eleven
Tokyu-Toyoko Line
Saikyou Line
Yamanote Line
MEIJI
Shibuya
7-Eleven
Fukushoji Temple
Ebisu Prime Square
DORI
渋谷区
SHIBUYA-KU
EBISUNISHI
River
Post office
ALLEGORY BUREAU
LAWSON
Tokyo Metro Hibiya Line
DAIKANYAMA STATION
ALLEGORY HOME TOOLS
PILE CAFE
LAWSON
MEIJI
7-Eleven
AFURI RAMEN
DORI
COCCA
FamilyMart
SAKANAYA EBISU-AN
FamilyMart
McDonald's
LAWSON
WILDLIFE TAILOR
Ebisu Park
EBISU STATION
EBISU
DORI
Post office
Tokyo Metro Hibiya Line
KOMAZAWA
7-Eleven
Natural LAWSON
Post office
LAWSON
N
EBISUMINAMI
KAPITAL
SENMYOJI TEMPLE
目黒区
MEGURO-KU
Yebisu Garden Place
7-Eleven
SHOSENJI TEMPLE
HINONE MIZUNONE
DUFFLE WITH KAPITAL
Post office
Tokyo Kyosai Hospital
National Institute for Defense Studies
TOKYO METROPOLITAN MUSEUM OF PHOTOGRAPHY
Nakameguro Park
0   100 m
Post office
Meguro
YAMATE
MITA
River
DORI
7-Eleven

1.

DUFFLE WITH KAPITAL

2-24-2 Ebisu Minami, Shibuya-ku
5768 1965
www.kapital.jp
Open Mon–Sun 11am–8pm
Ebisu station, West exit

Prepare to enter a brave new world of repurposed vintage clothing. Duffle with Kapital's rabbit-warren-like rooms are stuffed to the rafters with a mishmash of '60s and '70s Americana. The style is Navajo desert meets army surplus meets Woodstock, and the store's vibe is downbeat hippie, with burning incense, Jimmy Hendrix posters, buffalo skulls and old gas masks, but with a very Japanese aesthetic. Army fatigues are reimagined as suits and coats, ponchos and bags are patched with vintage Japanese fabric, and Native Americana gear and animal skins are all restructured. The clothes might be old, but what's happening to them is very, very new. It's shabby chic raised to the level of haute couture. Nearby sister store **Kapital** has a similar Americana/Tokyo/hippie aesthetic and also stocks inventive denim jeans, jackets and bags. We guarantee you won't have seen anything quite like these cutting-edge Ebisu stores. The clothing is inspiring and challenging, yet surprisingly wearable.

ALLEGORY HOME TOOLS

1-32-29 Ebisunishi, Shibuya-ku
3496 1516
Open Thurs–Tues 12–8pm
Daikanyama station

Allegory Home Tools sells everyday items that are not content to be just 'things'. Instead the objects in this store feel like they're saying: 'Hey! I know you use me every day, but that doesn't mean I can't be special'. The store's tasteful selection includes items for the kitchen, bathroom, dining room, living room and garden that all stay within a price range of ¥999 to ¥5000. You'll find ceramics, utensils and traditional Japanese items like tea whisks, kettles, rice bowls and teacups all sourced for their aesthetic appeal. Make sure you say hello to the resident budgie on your way in, and don't miss sister store **Allegory Bureau**, which applies the same 'special-thing' philosophy to stationery and office wares. You'll find it five minutes away on foot, around the corner in Daikanyama.

3.

WILDLIFE TAILOR

1-32-12 Ebisunishi, Shibuya-ku
5728 6320
Open Mon–Sun 11am–8pm
Ebisu station, West exit

A sign out the front of this shop boasts 'Best clothing store in the known universe!'. While there's no doubt some humour intended, this is also a statement of intent as this men's tailor brings back the attention to detail you'd expect from a shop of yesteryear. The green exterior with pot plants and retro signage might take you back to the days of the British Empire, but you won't get a safari suit or pith helmet here. What you will get is a great range of suits, shoes, polo shirts and jeans that will help you stand out in the urban jungle. Prowl around the two levels of clothes set amongst pot plants, oddments and antiques to discover an English gentleman's style put together with Japanese know-how.

COCCA

1-31-13 Ebisunishi, Shibuya-ku
3463 7681
Open Tues–Sun 11am–9pm
Daikanyama station

Just off the main drag, Cocca's white modernist building sits among a flourishing garden in a semi-residential part of Ebisu. When you enter it's like you've been invited into someone's home to see their immaculate textile collection, which the streamlined interior allows to speak for itself. The emphasis here is on nurturing new talent, and the expertise of local artisans is truly on display. You'll find intricate handmade fabrics (the heavy linen is exquisite), and designs that are bold and contemporary, or abstract updates on traditional motifs. Dressmakers can grab armfuls of material, while crafters can get hold of handy small offcuts. Cocca's mission statement is to drape everything in fabric, and after you've dropped by you'll definitely want to wrap yourself and your house in these beautiful textiles.

5.

AFURI RAMEN

1-1-7 Ebisu, Shibuya-ku
5795 0750
Open Mon–Sun 11am–5pm
Ebisu station, East exit

This ramen joint selling wonderful, intensely flavoured noodle soups is just a hop, skip and a jump from Ebisu station. It's in-and-out dining – no lingering here! – so slip some money into the vending machine to order your meal on the way in (there's English), pick your ramen, choose your noodle type and grab a seat at the counter. You can customise your dish if you like; we recommend adding extra crispy nori sheets. If you find ramen a bit heavy, get the speciality, the delicious yuzu broth; this citrus fruit creates a light and tangy dish that will leave you wanting more. For those of you who don't eat pork, the broth is made of chicken and you can ask for it without pork slices. Whatever you end up ordering, take a cue from your neighbours and slurp it to your heart's content.

HINONE MIZUNONE

39F, 4-20-30 Yebisu Garden
Place, Ebisu, Shibuya-ku
5793 7600
Open Mon–Sun 11am–2.30pm
& 5–11pm
Ebisu station, East exit

Ride the vertigo-inducing lift up to the 39th floor of Yebisu Garden Place to uncover this elegant Japanese restaurant. You're almost up in the clouds here and there's an amazing and free view of Tokyo's staggering sprawl. Slip off your shoes and head inside the beautiful traditional-style room to sample homemade tofu and free-range chicken blistered on the charcoal grill. At ¥2400 to ¥4700 for dinner it's well priced, but the lunchtime set boxes, with fresh sashimi, grilled meats, perfectly made rice and delicate tempura are an absolute steal at ¥950 to ¥1900. A fun thing to do here is to order a sake that overflows from its shot glass into a small box – drink first from the glass, then the box! Make the most of the view up here – on a clear day you can see Mount Fuji!

PILE CAFE

2F, 1-8-2 Ebisunishi, Shibuya-ku
3770 2615
Open Mon–Fri 11.30am–12am,
Sat–Sun 12pm–4am
Ebisu station, West exit

One look at Pile Cafe's curved, low-lit '70s windows will make you want to get yourself inside this ultra-cool yet cosy and unpretentious second-floor den. Seek out the entrance, climb the secret stairway and feel right at home among the retro velour and leather couches. It's best at night, when the soft yellow light from candles and vintage lamps softens the low tables, plush chairs, palm trees and oddball art. Groups of chatty locals sink into the seductive furniture and down drinks and delicious cake. The food extends to pastas and desserts, and there's an extensive list of classic cocktails. Add some extra yen for two hangover-inducing hours of all-you-can-drink booze. If you're after a coffee, this is the best place to spike it with that little something extra.

8

SAKANAYA EBISU-AN

1-8-3 Ebisunishi, Shibuya-ku
3770 7032
Open Mon–Fri 7pm–5am,
Sat–Sun 4pm–5am
Ebisu station, West exit

Ask for a 'booth' table out the back at this knockabout izakaya, best known for its seafood. While these tables are separated by thickly woven fabric partitions, that doesn't stop the noise as the rowdy after-work crowd pours in to order plates of excellent sashimi, grilled fish, scallops and hunger-busting fried chicken. Its unusual take on sushi – spheres of rice covered in delicate slices of fish and shiso leaves (a type of mint) – is a real treat. Wash everything down with some fine local beer or our favourite, the Okinawan umeshu, a delicious and potent drink with the sweet taste of burnt sugar. If you're feeling extra thirsty, get the set-price, all-you-can-drink menu (available in English, as is the food menu), which gives you a couple of hours to kill some brain cells.

TOKYO TIP
Don't miss the excellent
Tokyo Metropolitan
Museum of Photography at
Yebisu Garden Place.

French pastry shops and high-end fashion boutiques bring a feeling of luxe to this quiet neighbourhood, but fledgling Tokyo designers, vintage and craft stores, and indie galleries dotted around the backstreets ensure it also has street cred. The influx of young Tokyoites on weekends adds to the vibrant scene.

Meet your friends at Daikanyama station's south exit, a popular spot for daytrippers to kick off their hunt for great vintage gear and homewares before lounging the afternoon away in the area's hip cafes and bars.

DAIKANYAMA

SHOP
1 Nimes
2 Carboots
3 Tsumori Chisato
4 Junie Moon

SHOP, EAT AND DRINK
5 T-Site

EAT
6 Isshin
7 Soso

EAT AND DRINK
8 Tatemichiya

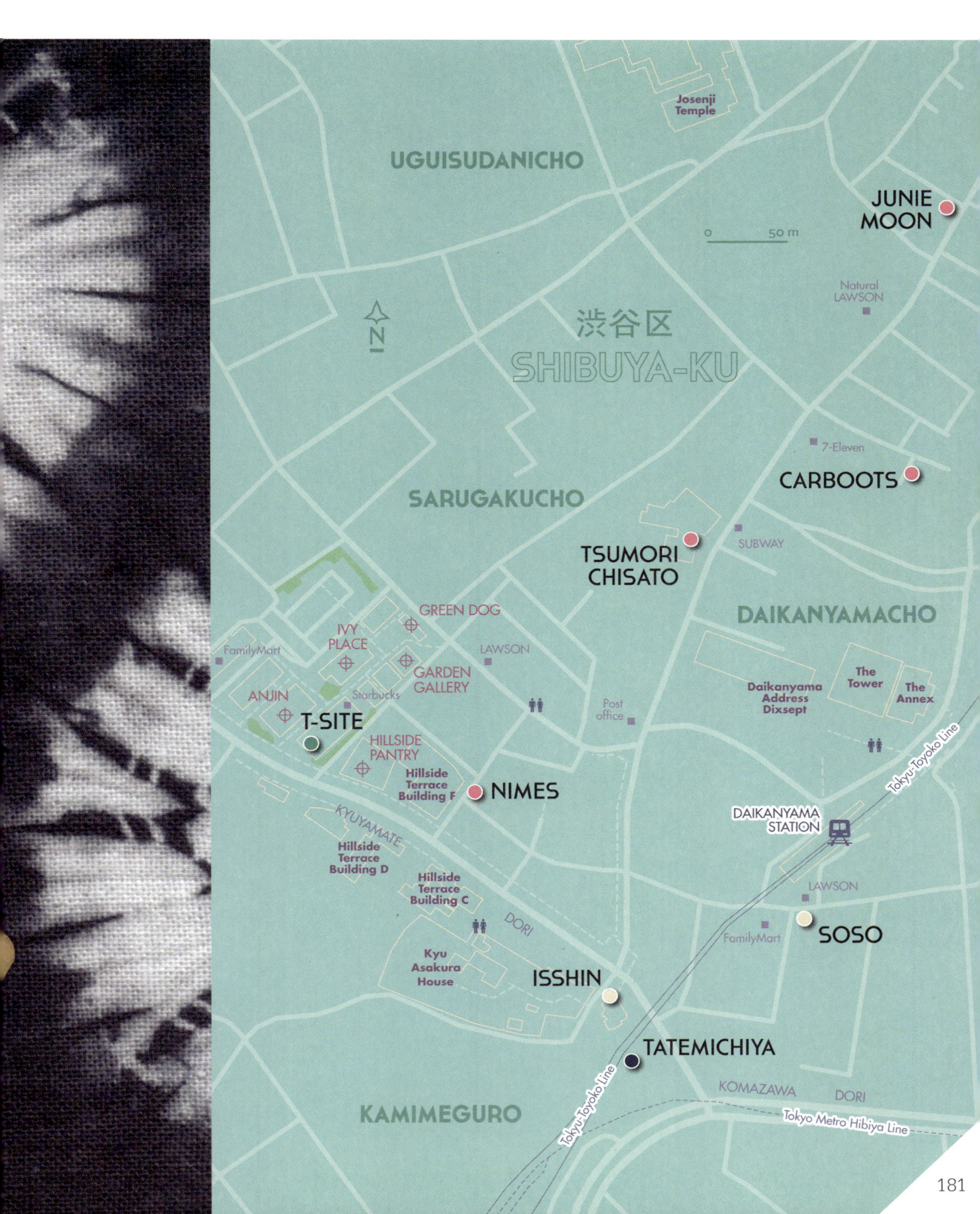

Josenji Temple
UGUISUDANICHO
0   50 m
JUNIE MOON
Natural LAWSON
N
渋谷区
SHIBUYA-KU
7-Eleven
CARBOOTS
SARUGAKUCHO
SUBWAY
TSUMORI CHISATO
DAIKANYAMACHO
GREEN DOG
IVY PLACE
FamilyMart
LAWSON
The Tower
The Annex
Daikanyama Address Dixsept
GARDEN GALLERY
ANJIN
Starbucks
Post office
T-SITE
HILLSIDE PANTRY
Hillside Terrace Building F
NIMES
Tokyu-Toyoko Line
KYUYAMATE
DAIKANYAMA STATION
Hillside Terrace Building D
Hillside Terrace Building C
LAWSON
DORI
SOSO
FamilyMart
Kyu Asakura House
ISSHIN
TATEMICHIYA
Tokyu-Toyoko Line
KOMAZAWA
DORI
KAMIMEGURO
Tokyo Metro Hibiya Line

NIMES

1F, 26-11 Sarugakucho,
Shibuya-ku
3463 0526
Open Mon–Sun 11.30am–7pm
Daikanyama station

Tokyo is in love with Paris, and Nimes is a love letter to all things French. It's been around for 20 years, and in that time it hasn't strayed from its Francophile roots, excelling in the timeless styles of French provincial and nautical chic fashion. The outfits are cute and elegant at the same time, often drawing on classic lines but with the echoes of yesteryear given a contemporary flair. Quaint linen dresses, delicate floral slips, classic striped tops, ballet shoes and berets are all updated for the modern girl about town. Pop upstairs for coats and cardigans, or stroll a few stores up the street for a more informal selection and some downright adorable baby gear.

CARBOOTS

14-5 Daikanyamacho,
Shibuya-ku
3464 6868
Open Mon–Sun 12–9pm
Daikanyama station

Down a quiet lane away from foot traffic, you'll find this off-the-grid retro store that specialises in European 'antique' vintage. The buyers here have a meticulous eye: expect a tasteful collection of jewellery, handbags, quaint sailor dresses, French '60s chic and pre-loved boots and shoes. Some of the clothing is quite rare, including some exquisite lace and linen, which is worth paying a bit extra for. Look closely among the racks and you'll find some real treasures, like the tiny '20s French dolls, complete with movable limbs. Elsewhere there are ashtrays, badges, matchboxes, French pop records, Beatles paraphernalia and all sorts of other trinkets and relics from a romantic bygone age. If you were lucky enough to find any of this stuff at an actual car-boot sale, it would be the greatest day of your life.

TSUMORI CHISATO

1F, La Fuente, 11-1 Sarugakucho, Shibuya-ku
5728 3225
www.tsumorichisato.com
Open Mon–Sun 11am–8pm
Daikanyama station

Tsumori Chisato is a darling of the Japanese fashion and design scenes. She's admired for her garment constructions that push traditional boundaries and her unexpected use of clashing patterns, textures, shapes and colours. Chisato's Daikanyama store displays her imaginative creations, flights of fancy that start out as illustrations and end up as beautiful designs. The store's displays are as interesting and playful as the clothing: trees sprout from the walls, giant tigers prowl around and there are regular eye-catching in-store installations, many of which are cat themed. Shoppers here tend to be young creatives with a vivid imagination; the cat-themed range of clothing also pulls in those who want to 'cute up' their wardrobe. If the outfits don't fit into your budget, grab one of the iconic cat phone covers or t-shirts.

JUNIE MOON

1F, Suzuen Daikanyama Building,
4-3 Sarugaku-cho, Shibuya-ku
www.juniemoon.jp
Open Tues–Sun 11am–9pm
Daikanyama station

Blythe is a fashion doll like no other. Her oversized head, massive eyes, super cuteness and to-die-for wardrobe have spawned an army of obsessive collectors. Junie Moon is a mecca for Blythe's many fans and serves as a catwalk for the much-loved doll to rock her latest styles. You can spend hours here hunting through brightly coloured boxes for vintage 'skate date' or 'bohemian beats' outfits for your dolly, or you can catch up on the latest-release Blythe models, one-offs and exclusives. The store even hosts 'Salon de Junie Moon', a monthly workshop with hands-on instruction for how to make your own Blythe outfits. Devotees will also want to stock up on stationery, tote bags and other Blythe-related items. It's almost impossible not to smile along with the young, overexcited clientele.

T-SITE

17-5 Sarugakucho, Shibuya-ku
3770 2525
Open Mon–Sun 7am–2am
Daikanyama station

So much more than a bookstore, this biosphere dedicated to all things peruse-worthy has become a magnet for bibliophiles and weekend browsers alike. T-Site has an absurdly extensive range of books of every genre, including a large selection of English releases. One of the big drawcards is 'Magazine Street', which boasts around 30,000 vintage magazines (mostly from the 1960s and '70s), as well as the latest publications.

T-Site also stocks well over 100,000 CDs and DVDs (staff will even burn previously unavailable classics to disc for you!). Awesome workstations and reading sections turn the landmark building into a mini library, and on the second floor you can leaf through a book at the excellent cafe **Anjin**. And that's not all folks! Within the grounds there's a camera store with a Leica museum, a dog-grooming salon and **Ivy Place**, a hugely popular cafe and bar. You could easily lose a day in this mega-complex, and on Sundays hordes of Tokyoites do just that.

ISSHIN

B1F, 30-3 Sarugakucho,
Shibuya-ku
6455 1614
Open Mon–Sun 11am–4pm &
5pm–12am
Daikanyama station

Shhhhh! Don't let the secret out. Even most Tokyoites don't know about this fantastic rice-specialist restaurant that's hidden down a discreet stairway. Needless to say, you'll be dining with in-the-know locals. There's little English spoken and no English at all on the menu, but take a punt on anything and you're unlikely to be disappointed. Isshin is serious about rice and has seriously good lunch sets that will only set you back between ¥980 and ¥1600. Vegetarians should get the tamago special, a delicious slab of omelette with miso and salad. All lunch sets come with rice in a beautiful bamboo box, and the staff will happily refill the rice for free if you want more. Check out the 3D prints of straw on the fabric chairs, which bring a real sense of fun to the upscale room.

7.

SOSO

1-34-28, Daikanyamacho,
Shibuya-ku
6416 9827
www.soso-tokyo.com
Open Mon–Sun
11.30am–2.30pm &
6pm–12am (teahouse);
2.30–5pm (cafe)
Daikanyama station

Shopping in Daikanyama is an exhausting business, so you'll need to refuel at some point. Enter Soso, which functions as both a cafe and teahouse, and – let's just get this out of the way right now – has nothing at all so-so about it. For under ¥1500 you'll get a lunch of somen noodles (like vermicelli but made with wheat) with a rice ball and vegetables, or the rice set complete with dish of the day. The main drawcard here is the otenmae set, which lets you take control of your own simple tea ceremony. You're provided with hot water, matcha (milled green tea) and a wooden whisk, so you can get to it and whisk your own blend. Complement the tea with some of Soso's dangos: delicious, sweet rice-flour dumplings.

8.

TATEMICHIYA

B1F, 30-8 Sarugakucho,
Shibuya-ku
5459 3431
Open Mon–Fri 6pm–4am,
Sat–Sun 6pm–12am
Daikanyama station

Hey ho, let's go! The fun kicks off at night in this grungy izakaya, a magnet for provocative, art-conscious locals, hang-abouts and rock 'n' roll diehards. Expect Sex Pistols and Ramones posters and a soundtrack of punk, rock and punk rock, turned up to 11. Pop artist Yoshitomo Nara loves it here; check out his handiwork on the walls at the back and Mick Jagger's signature on the front wall near the entrance. The honest izakaya fare includes delicious grilled skewers of meat, and atsuage (deep-fried tofu) that people cross town for. Be brave and add some natto (fermented soybeans) to your meal; you'll either hate or handle this stinky bean. Your host will be cheerfully singing along to the music while pouring your sake. Tatemichiya is unpretentious and its food delicious, and as a result Daikanyama's cool kids and faded rockers come here in droves.

7.
8.
TOKYO TIP
Daikanyama is within
walking distance of
Ebisu, Nakameguro
and Shibuya.

Midori Sakai sells textiles and apparel. She was born in Tohoku in Japan, but has lived in Tokyo for nine years. In her spare time she loves cooking, listening to music, going to museums and shopping. She loves Tokyo!

How do you define Tokyo style?

I would call it original. I think people in Tokyo have many styles and they really enjoy dressing up. I spend many exciting days in Tokyo just looking at different people's fashion. I love Tokyo style.

Where do you like to eat and drink in Daikanyama?

Tatemichiya (*see* p. 188) is a Japanese pub where the food and drinks are excellent and the music and people are loud and friendly. I recommend lunch at Chachamaru; I often have the shokado (premium) bento. I also buy bread at Hillside Pantry (*see* map p. 181) once a week.

Where do you go for a
quick escape from Tokyo?

I go to my hometown, Tohoku,
on the Shinkansen (bullet train).
I like to see my family and there
is some beautiful nature there.
Or I go to Kamakura on the train;
it's my favourite daytrip place. It
is not far away, is very peaceful
and has a giant Buddha and
nice beaches.

This low-rise bohemian precinct's canal is one of the most festive spots in Tokyo to celebrate the arrival of the famous cherry blossoms. It's fringed with hip places to eat, drink and shop, including a row of izakayas and French eateries overlooking the water.

Strolling along the canal and around Nakameguro's backstreets on weekends is an absolute joy. It's hard to believe you're only minutes away from high-rise madness. The precinct is busy making a name for itself as a go-to place for handcrafts, revamped vintage wares and edgy cafes and restaurants. Keep an eye out for much-hyped pizza and coffee places; new ones seem to pop up almost daily.

Saigoyama Park
AOBADAI
KYUYAMATE
DORI
KYUYAMATE
LAWSON
Starbucks
T-SITE
Post office
目黒区
MEGURO-KU
Kyu Askura House
Tokyu-Toyoko Line
DORI
COW BOOKS
MAHAKALA'S HAPPY PUDDING
7-Eleven
YAMATE
FamilyMart
Meguro
DORI
YAMATE
1LDK
SATO SAKURA MUSEUM
DORI
RED BOOK
7-Eleven
FamilyMart
Starbucks
KAMIMEGURO
Tokyo Metro Hibiya Line
COLOBOCKLE
NAKAMEGURO STATION
E
7-Eleven
KOMAZAWA
7-Eleven
Starbucks
7-Eleven
AKIRA
YAMATE
Tokyu-Toyoko Line
Post office
NAKAMEGURO
DORI
DORI
River
Meguro Riverside Park
PATISSERIE POTAGER
POTAGER MARCHE
N
J'ANTIQUES
KOMAZAWA
Shogakuji Temple
KA-KU-RA
0   100 m

1LDK

1-8-28 Kamimeguro, Meguro-ku
3780 1645
Open Mon–Sun 10am–5pm
Nakameguro station

Away from the canal in residential Nakameguro, 1LDK is making its own scene with an effortlessly cool men's fashion concept store that has all the locals talking. Owner Takayuki Minami is here to make your every day, well, less everyday with a range of up-to-the-minute men's clothing, accessories, stationery, glasses and whatever else he deems worthy. (Incidentally, this was the best selection of men's spectacles we saw in Tokyo.) The stylish store retains its original look and feel, as does its older sibling across the street, which sells mostly womenswear and homewares, and has an excellent cafe and bookstore.

2

COLOBOCKLE

1-1-54 Nakameguro, Meguro-ku
3714 7393
www.colobockle.jp
Open Mon–Sun 12–7pm
Nakameguro station

Surely the cutest shop in existence, Colobockle is a must-visit for fans of illustration. Set in a beautiful old Japanese house, it's like entering an imaginary wonderland of parading, cavorting animals. Illustrator Michiko Tachimoto's colourful, folky characters peer out from posters, dangle from mobiles hanging from the ceiling and also decorate ceramics and stationery. The wonderful Colobockle calendar makes a great souvenir; its pandas, pink hippos, elephants with patchwork ears and cheeky monkeys will bring a smile to your dial every day. Similar characters come to life in Colobockle's animated DVD, which is guaranteed to cheer. Little ones will love the range of children's books and stationery, and no-one will be immune to the shop's contagious fun.

3.

J'ANTIQUES

2-25-13 Kamimeguro, Meguro-ku
5704 8188
Open Mon–Sun 12–10pm
Nakameguro station

J'Antiques is an essential pit stop while browsing the stores on Nakameguro's amazing shotengai (shopping street). You're unlikely to walk past without noticing it, as the rustic furniture stacked out the front is super eye-catching. Inside you'll find a captivating mix of salvaged items that lean towards Americana, including a quality selection of vintage men's and women's clothing, fabric and accessories. The great line in pre-loved denim is especially worth checking out. Perhaps the biggest drawcard here though is the selection of curios. Second-hand buttons, pins, signage, lights and boxes will have you foraging for hours.

4.

COW BOOKS

1-14-11 Aobadai, Meguro-ku
5459 1747
www.cowbooks.jp
Open Tues–Sun 1–9pm
Nakameguro station

The staff at Cow Books love their tomes so much they actually take them on daytrips back to the forest 'where they came from'. Seriously. This left-of-centre bookstore specialises in out-of-print books, mostly from the '50s and '60s, and the underground press. Its selection will take you on a journey through social politics, the beat generation, the hippie subculture of San Francisco's Haight-Ashbury, black power, art theory, music and poetry. If you feel the need to start a revolution or a new social movement, you'll find something here to show you how! Counterculture authors like Timothy Leary and William S. Burroughs lead the way, but you can also grab first editions by lesser known modern authors.

5.

MAHAKALA'S HAPPY PUDDING

1-17-5, Aoba Maison 101,
Aobadai, Meguro-ku
6427 8706
Open Mon–Sun 11am–6pm
Nakameguro station

This hole-in-the-wall spot on a street along the canal sells glorious hits of creamy egg custard that come in tiny glass pots. The flavours range from the delicious classic caramel to the equally good matcha, a green-tea custard for those who like their sweets a little less sweet but with a whole lot of interesting. Then there's the black sesame, the honey lemon, the chestnut chocolate pudding, the tiramisu … oh excuse me, I just went to pudding heaven in my mind … If you can't decide what to choose, look for the number one on the menu (which indicates the best-selling item). Whatever you pick, you can't go wrong at ¥350 to ¥400 a pot. Staff politely request that you recycle the takeaway pots, but taking them home and using them as vases is the same thing, right?

6.

PATISSERIE POTAGER

2-44-9 Kamimeguro, Meguro-ku
6279 7753
Open Mon–Sun 10am–8pm
Nakameguro station

If your preferred way of eating your greens is through the medium of cake, Patisserie Potager is the place for you. Mind-boggling flavours like blueberry and pumpkin tart, zucchini roll cake and passionfruit and pepper chiffon actually taste quite delicious. The edamame (green soybean) cheesecake might be stretching it, but this is certainly the place to experiment. Make sure you get the 'veggie suites' (geddit?), a takeaway gift box that you might end up gifting to yourself. Why not? The treats not only taste good, but are also thought to have medicinal properties. If you're more into savoury, don't despair. **Potager Marche** just down the road is a great place to experience all-vegetable sushi and veggie bento boxes.

5.
6.
www.happypudding.com
TOKYO TIP
To find out more about
cherry blossoms, visit the
Sato Sakura Museum.
Potager
Potager
Potager
Rucola jelly & black sesame with soy milk mousse
ルッコラゼリー＆黒ゴマ豆乳ムース
¥39
野菜の味 ★★★
甘さ ★
ヘルシー ★★★
Buckwheat milk tea jelly with ginger
そば茶のジンジャーミルクティゼリー
¥410 (税込)

AKIRA

1-10-23 Nakameguro,
Meguro-ku
3793 0051
Open Mon–Sun 5pm–3am
Nakameguro station

If you're looking for one of the best izakaya experiences in Tokyo, Akira will fit the brief. A hidden gem, it's in a stunning old-school building at the end of a tiny strip overlooking the canal. The interior is beautiful, traditional and rustic, and the scent of smoke and grilled meats wafts over you on arrival. It's great fun grilling your own meat at your table, but the chicken tartare in ponzu (a citrus-based sauce) is what most people come here for. We also recommend the fried chicken skin, which is as delicious and wonderfully bad for you as it sounds. Make sure you book, as it's deservedly popular and gets busy quickly, especially on weekends. Pull up a cushion on the bamboo floor for the best views, then sit back with a draught beer or a plum wine.

KA-KU-RA

2-42-13 Kamimeguro,
Meguro-ku
3710 0299
Open Wed–Mon 12–1.30pm
& 6–11.30pm
Nakameguro station

Chef Aichi Sugiyama studied home economics and Chinese medicine, and as a result the macrobiotic curries he makes at Ka-Ku-Ra are packed with medicinal herbs that might just cure what ails you. The restaurant's rough-and-tumble, laid-back charm draws the crowds, as do the delicious, well-priced curries. Expect yours to be spiked with ginseng, leaves of angelica or totonoeru (which, incidentally, helps to regulate the flow of gas …). As with all Japanese curries, it's a good idea to opt for a few extras: egg, avocado and fried vegetables will add an interesting dimension for an additional ¥450 or so. The food can run out quickly so time your run, especially at lunch when the window for ordering is only an hour and a half. Ask for some beer or sake if you like, although that might undo all the benefits of those medicinal herbs …

Michiko Tachimoto wanted to create her own children's books since she was in kindergarten. She displays her illustrated books and artwork in her shop Colobockle (*see* p. 195), which she opened with her husband ten years ago to showcase her work, a mix of hand-sewn craft and collage illustration.

What makes Japanese illustration special?

This is a difficult question to answer. I'm not sure that I believe Japanese illustration is more special than in other countries, but it does have its own unique feel.

What is your favourite thing in your shop?

I like the shop itself! The old and small house that my husband and I renovated with our friends. We hope our customers feel like they are in a fairytale world.

Where do you like to eat and drink in Nakameguro?

I go to Red Book (*see* map p. 193), near our shop. I love the chicken curry. It's a small cafe, but so comfortable. I also recommend it at night when it turns into a great bar.

Where do you go for a quick escape from Tokyo?

I like to go to Karuizawa in Nagano. It takes little more than an hour to reach from Tokyo by Shinkansen (bullet train). I like spending time leisurely strolling amongst nature. There are various outdoor activities to enjoy, such as hiking and cycling in summer, and skiing and ice-skating in winter.

www.colobockle.jp

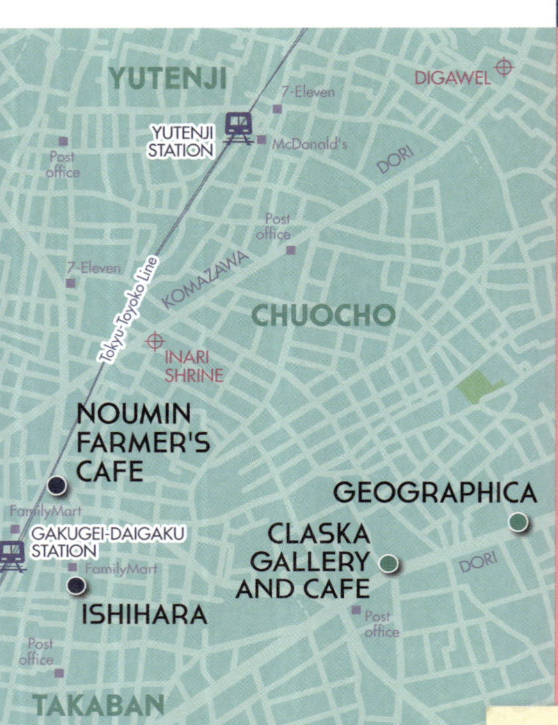

MEGURO AND GAKUGEI-DAIGAKU

Fondly known as 'interior street' for its abundance of furniture and homewares stores, sweeping Meguro Dori links these two creative neighbourhoods. To the north-east of the bustling Meguro precinct's station you'll find parks, gardens, teahouses and in-the-know shopping opportunities. West of the station, there's a covered arcade crammed with pocket-sized old-world eateries, while hip new bars and coffee houses are sprouting around the river.

Gakugei-Daigaku has much more of a residential neighbourhood feel, with plenty of quaint restaurants and great little shopping finds amongst its patchwork of tiny streets.

24   JUN 80T6

SHOP
1 MINÄ PERHONEN
2 ARKISTOT

SHOP, EAT AND DRINK
3 Geographica
4 Chum Apartment
5 Claska Gallery and Cafe

17

EAT
6 Switch Coffee
EAT AND DRINK
7 Noumin Farmer's Cafe
8 Shin One and Two
9 Ishihara

TOKYO METROPOLITAN MUSEUM OF PHOTOGRAPHY
Westin Tokyo
MATSUOKA MUSEUM OF ART
Institute of Medical Science University of Tokyo
MEGURO
港区
MINATO-KU
MEGURO-KU
目黒区
ARKISTOT
SHIROKANEDAI STATION
SWITCH COFFEE
Tokyo Metropolitan Teien Art Museum
MINÄ PERHONEN
7-Eleven
FamilyMart
SHIN ONE AND TWO
Saikyou Line
Yamanote Line
FamilyMart
Mita - Line &
Nambuku - Line
DORI
KAMIOSAKI
TO NOUMIN FARMER'S CAFE, ISHIHARA, CLASKA GALLERY AND CAFE & GEOGRAPHICA
(SEE MAP LEFT)
7-Eleven
KUME MUSEUM OF ART
Starbucks
MEGURO
Post office
7-Eleven
MEGURO STATION
MEGURO ROUTE
DAIENJI TEMPLE
Ikedayama Park
CHUM APARTMENT
YAMATE DORI
Post office
HIGASHIGOTANDA
Meguro
SUGINO GAKUEN COSTUME MUSEUM
Yamanote Line
SHIMOMEGURO
0   200 m
Saikyou Line
FamilyMart
Tokyu Meguro Line
LAWSON
FamilyMart
River
7-Eleven
NO 2
FamilyMart
YAMATE
7-Eleven
LAWSON
LAWSON
E
LAWSON
E
Post office
GOTANDA STATION
E
DORI
McDonald's
FamilyMart
Post office
7-Eleven
FamilyMart
Post office
7-Eleven
EXPRESSWAY
FUDO-MAE STATION
FamilyMart
N
Tokyu Meguro Line
FamilyMart
DORI
7-Eleven
LAWSON
SAKURADA
OSAKIHIROKOJI STATION
YAMATE
品川区
SHINAGAWA-KU
METROPOLITAN
Post office
Toei Asakusa Line
Tokyo Ikegami Line
7-Eleven
DORI
Post office

MINÄ PERHONEN

3F, 5-18-17 Shirokanedai,
Minato-ku
5420 3766
www.mina-perhonen.jp
Open Tues–Sun 12–8pm
Meguro station, East exit

Designer Akira Minagawa's drawings and patterns are inspired by his passion for Finland. Indeed, his fashion and textile brand Minä Perhonen has its origins in the Finnish language: 'minä' means 'I' and 'perhonen' is 'butterfly'. As such, Minagawa's designs, as much art as they are fashion, mimic the delicate and timeless beauty of a butterfly's wing. The brand is well known and coveted by anyone into fabric creation, print techniques and meticulous textiles, and this Minä Perhonen clothing store, located on a quiet Meguro backstreet, is the flagship. (There are other stores in Kyoto and Matsumoto.)

Head up the stairs and float through the shop; its warm woods, soft lights and small library of illustration and design books make it the perfect showcase for the beautiful clothes. Minagawa created the staff uniforms for the recently opened Tokyo Skytree building, a sure sign that the Minä Perhonen brand is held in high esteem.

ARKISTOT

2F & 3F, 5-13-14 Shirokanedai, Minato-ku
5475 3837
Open Tues–Sun 12–8pm
Meguro station, East exit

You'll find Arkistot just a short stroll down from Minä Perhonen (*see* opposite page). If you fancy sewing up your own storm, you can buy Minä Perhonen fabrics here. It also sells covetable homewares, and beautiful children's and baby clothes. There's a showcase of the best Minä Perhonen pieces from past collections too. If you're looking for a keepsake, the glassware and ceramics are exquisite, and the tiny butterfly badges and incense holders are adorable.

3.

GEOGRAPHICA

1-25-20 Naka, Meguro-ku
5773 1145
Open Mon–Sun 11am–8pm
Gakugei-Daigaku station,
East exit

If you love sifting through antiques, oddments and ephemera from days gone by, Geographica's three storeys of antique whimsy will be your idea of a great day out.

Mahogany and walnut furniture, lace bonnets, teddy bears and shelves of fine china sit alongside pre-loved European and Japanese books, matchboxes, magazines and badges from the '50s and '60s. Have a leaf through the old postcards: you never know, you might recognise a distant relative. On the second floor there's **Il Levante**, a gorgeous little Italian cafe set out like train compartments where you can take a break from all that rummaging. Locals and those who speak Japanese can take furniture restoration classes in the Geographica workshop.

CHUM APARTMENT

2-23-3 Shimomeguro,
Meguro-ku
3490 2921
Open Mon–Sat 12pm–12am,
Sun 12–7pm (bar and cafe);
Mon–Sun 12–8pm (shop)
Meguro station, West exit

Japanese artist Chiharu Yoshikawa took a run-down mansion on a quiet Meguro backstreet and turned it into local hot spot Chum (pronounced 'charm') Apartment. Look for the Kombi-like van parked out the front, a hint of the hippie traveller vibe that extends to the Moroccan colour palette inside this cafe-cum-bar-cum-shop. The peeling discoloured walls, iron latticework, crosses, skulls and low-lit chandeliers give the place an eerie feel, but the repurposed furniture and deep couches cosy things up. Grab a daily set lunch for ¥1100, including coffee or tea, then head up to **Mucha** on the second floor, a shop selling rustic handmade ceramics. It's open late, so come back at night, slip into one of the nooks and crannies in the cafe-bar, order a wine, beer or shochu (distilled spirit) and make like a local.

CLASKA GALLERY AND CAFE

1-3-18 Chuocho, Meguro-ku
3719 8123
www.claska.com
Open Mon–Sun 11am–7pm
(shop and gallery);
7.30am–12am (cafe)
Gakugei-Daigaku station,
East exit

It's a bit of a walk from the station, but Claska is one of Tokyo's, if not the world's, best boutique hotels. It's ultra stylish and yet unpretentious, a feat made possible by supreme attention to detail combined with friendly staff. If you don't happen to be staying here, there's still every reason to visit. Gallery shop **Do** is a sublimely curated selection of new Japanese design, craft and everyday items that you'll no doubt want to take home with you. Attached is a small gallery that shows regular exhibitions by local designers and illustrators. Cafe/restaurant **Kiokuh** is one of the city's coolest places to hang out. The pick of the menu is the Japanese breakfast, but it's also the perfect place for evening drinks or an afternoon coffee and cake while you watch pooches being pampered at the adjacent canine spa **Dogman**.

6

SWITCH COFFEE

1-17-23 Meguro, Meguro-ku
6420 3633
www.switchcoffeetokyo.com
Open Mon–Sun 10am–7pm
Meguro station, West exit

This hole-in-the-wall coffee stand is off the main strip but it's well worth the wander; everything about the place is done well. The exterior is stylish, and the row of coffee machines along the counter is a deft touch. This is a takeaway kind of joint, with no seats, but you can rest on a small wooden bench outside. Staff here are friendly and knowledgeable; they talk about coffee like it's fine wine, referring to regions, bean varieties and fruit aromas, and might suggest a particular blend has a hint of blueberry jam or an afterglow of sweet brown sugar. If a particular blend takes your fancy, you can buy beans in 250-gram packets to go. Terms like 'single origin' and 'Costa Rican dragon' can make you feel like you're getting your hands on something illicit, and the coffee is so darn good that you may as well be.

7

NOUMIN FARMER'S CAFE

2-21-4 Takaban, Meguro-ku
5734 1190
Open Mon–Sun 11am–11pm
Gakugei-Daigaku station,
East exit

Inside Noumin, a vegetarian cafe in a reworked old Japanese house, you'll hear running water and meditative music. There's a mishmash of furniture, some of which looks like it was found by the side of the road, while other pieces would probably sell for a fortune at Sotheby's. Noumin isn't called the Farmer's Cafe for nothing: the food here is rustic and straight from the land, not to mention simply delicious. The ¥1200 lunch set gets you soup, a drink and a main. We tried the vegetable platter, a tasting plate with a central mound of rice surrounded by nine beautifully prepared tofu and vegetable delights. Drinks include organic coffee, homemade plum wine and malt beer, and you needn't feel guilty about having dessert, because many of them are made from vegetables!

TOKYO TIP
The stroll along the canal from Meguro to Nakameguro is delightful in spring and autumn.

8

SHIN ONE AND TWO

1-5-19 Meguro, Meguro-ku
5298 5411
Open Mon–Sun 5pm–1am
Meguro station, West exit

A short stroll from the station down Meguro Dori will bring you to a strip of old-school ramen (noodle soup) joints and yakitori dens, which specialise in grilled skewered chicken. These eateries include Shin One and Shin Two, side-by-side, standing-only bars where you can prop yourself up and eat and drink like the locals and salarymen. The walls are plastered with food and drink menus written in kanji, while the actual menu is a kooky mix of meat, seafood and French cheese. (Just go with it – you won't be disappointed.) Wine at ¥450 per glass? Yes please. These fantastic-looking bars are perfect for snapping photos, although your pictures will likely become more blurry as the night progresses.

ISHIHARA

1F, 2-16-14 Takaban, Meguro-ku
6452 4016
Open Mon–Fri 11.30am–4pm
& 6pm–12am, Sat–Sun
11.30am–12am
Gakugei-Daigaku station,
East exit

If you're hunting for a delicious soba noodle lunch, check out Ishihara. It's a top-notch soba restaurant by day, but at night this eatery transforms into an izakaya, specialising in fare from the Edo period (1603–1867). The grilled fish fins with creamy mayonnaise are addictive and the deep-fried octopus in breadcrumbs is every bit as good as it sounds. For something unique and extra tasty, order the yanaka shouga, the young stem of the ginger plant. The sparkling sake was our beverage of choice from the extensive drinks menu. Finish off your meal with soba noodles just like they used to do in the good old days!

Ryo Komura was born and raised in Tokyo and has spent all of his life there. He previously worked in fashion apparel, but now works with textiles. Ryo is in charge of vintage items at Uguisu the Little Shoppe (*see* p. 66), and otherwise works in Meguro and lives in Gakugei-Daigaku.

What do you love about Japanese fabrics and textiles?

I love how each craftsman's handwork has its own colour shades and stitch tension, making each fabric unique and special. You don't get this so much from machine-made fabrics.

Where do you like to shop for clothes in Meguro/ Gakugei-Daigaku?

Digawel (*see* map p. 204) in Meguro is my favourite shop in this area. I love its store interior; it has a relaxed atmosphere and is bathed in natural light. Its shirts, all made in Japan, have shorter cuffs than other shirts, which makes it easy to roll up the sleeves. I like little touches like that.

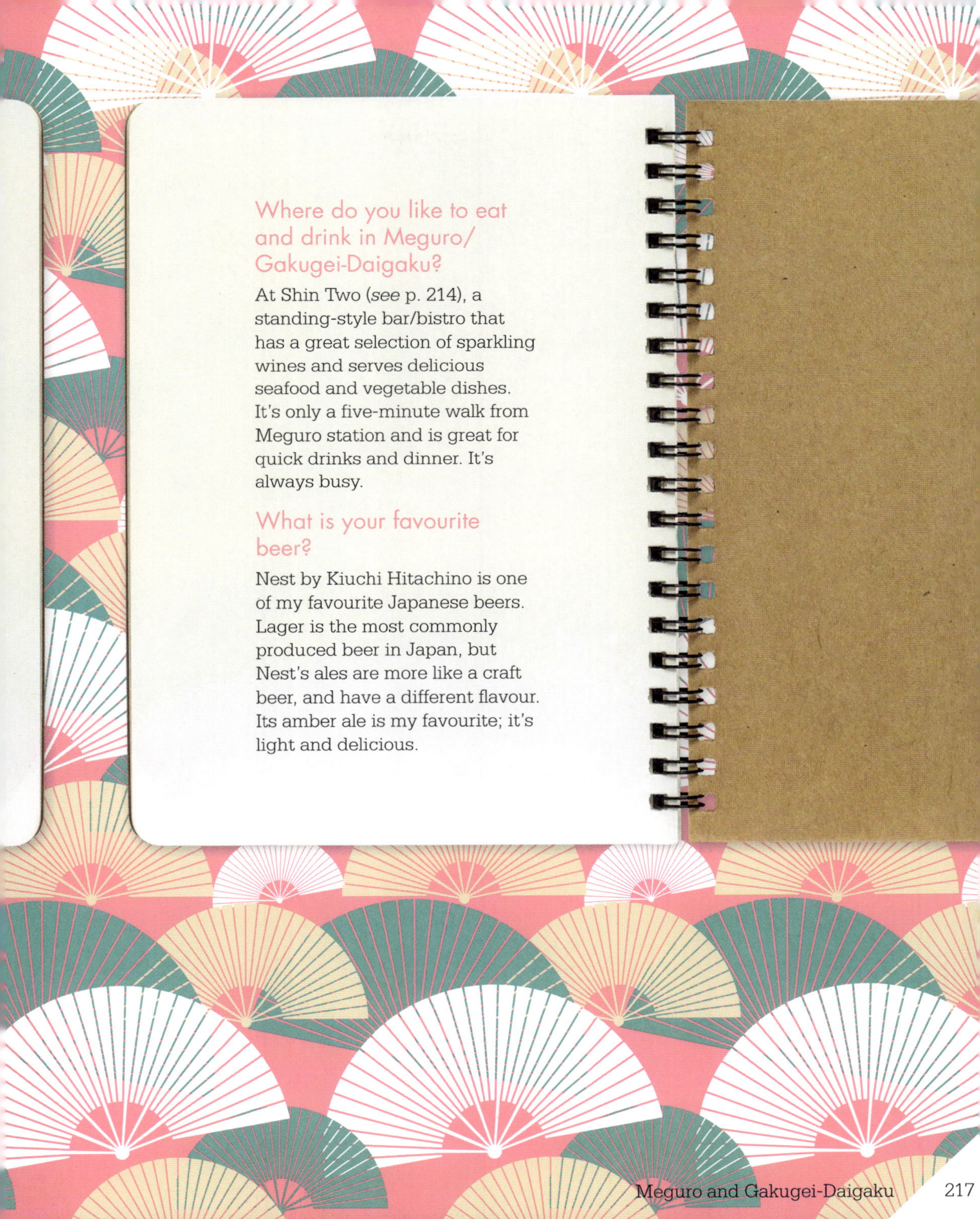

Where do you like to eat and drink in Meguro/ Gakugei-Daigaku?

At Shin Two (*see* p. 214), a standing-style bar/bistro that has a great selection of sparkling wines and serves delicious seafood and vegetable dishes. It's only a five-minute walk from Meguro station and is great for quick drinks and dinner. It's always busy.

What is your favourite beer?

Nest by Kiuchi Hitachino is one of my favourite Japanese beers. Lager is the most commonly produced beer in Japan, but Nest's ales are more like a craft beer, and have a different flavour. Its amber ale is my favourite; it's light and delicious.

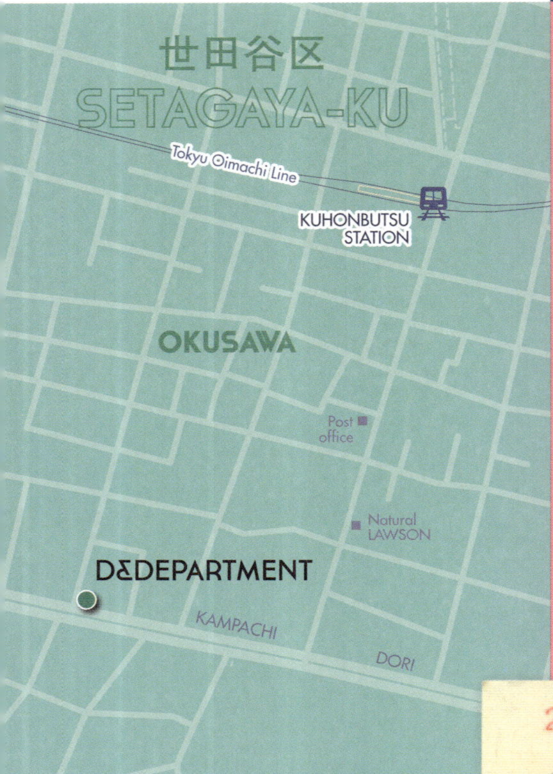

JIYUGAOKA AND KUHONBUTSU

Just minutes by train from Shibuya, lazy, breezy Jiyugaoka will make you feel like you've left the madness of the city far behind. Most shops go with a French theme here, so you won't be out of place if you hit Marie Claire Dori in a beret and Breton shirt walking a French bulldog. There's a plethora of vintage stores, handcraft shops and cafes visited by 20- and 30-somethings who seem to be on a permanent go-slow.

Go for an afternoon sashay alongside the train line through Jiyugaoka to Kuhonbutsu. Be sure not to miss one of Tokyo's best-kept secrets: the 800-year-old Kumano Shrine, a popular place to visit on a Sunday afternoon.

24

SHOP
1 Popeye
2 Tokyo Shobo
3 Check & Stripe

SHOP, EAT AND DRINK
4 D&Department

17

EAT
5 Baishinka Tea House

EAT AND DRINK
6 Jiyugaoka Burger

DRINK
7 Ra.a.g.f

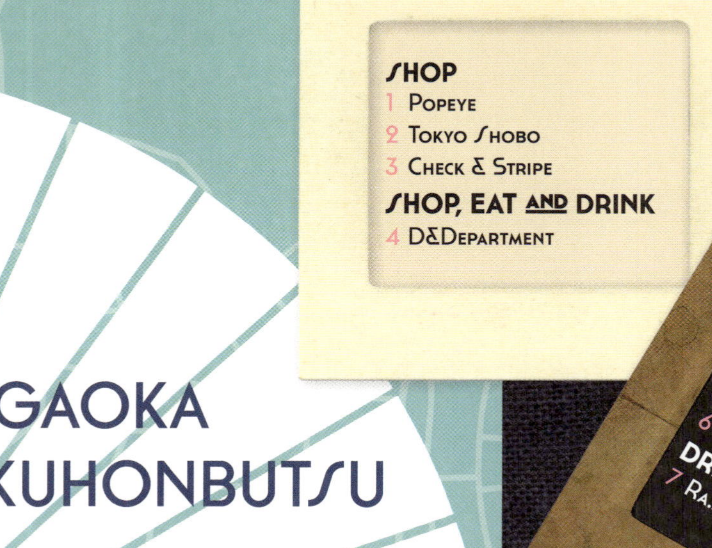

Tokoji Temple
HIKAWA SHRINE
FamilyMart
BAISHINKA TEA HOUSE
YAKUMO
JIYU
DORI
Post office
FUKASAWA
DORI
MEGURO
N
0   100 m
Natural LAWSON
MEGURO   DORI
JIYU
目黒区
MEGURO-KU
DORI
Tokyu-Toyoko Line
7-Eleven
KUMANO SHRINE
JIYUGAOKA
FamilyMart
RA.A.G.F
JIYUGAOKA BURGER
CHECK & STRIPE
LAWSON
POPEYE
Kuhonbutsu Joshinji Temple
LAWSON
7-Eleven
Post office
Starbucks
McDonald's
MARIE CLAIRE DORI
JIYUGAOKA STATION
TOKYO SHOBO
CAFE ONE
OKUSAWA
LAWSON
Tokyu Oimachi Line
KUHONBUTSU STATION
7-Eleven
Post office
OKUSAWA STATION
LAWSON
TO D&DEPARTMENT
(SEE MAP LEFT)
Tokyu-Toyoko Line
Tokyu-Meguro Line

1.

POPEYE

2-10-2 Jiyugaoka, Meguro-ku
3718 3431
Open Mon–Fri 11am–8.30pm
Jiyugaoka station, Central exit

Just 77 years young, this camera store has moved with the times. A DIY minilab, you can process your pics on the go here and then turn them into creative masterpieces. It's perfect for both photography enthusiasts and those just wanting to get a bit more hands-on with their happy snaps. Bring your preferred data storage device – the photo-machines here take USB, SD cards and CDs – or you can plug your phone straight in. Choose from different paper stocks and sizes, and then once you have your prints, pretty them up with the clever framing and mounting options. There are also stickers, stamps and tape if you want to decorate your album or portfolio, and boxes of colourful dangly knick-knacks to add personality to your camera. Check out the charming mix of antique and new cameras, maps, frames and photo albums while you're here.

TOKYO SHOBO

1-9-6 Marie Claire Dori,
Jiyugaoka, Meguro-ku
3718 2413
Open Mon–Sun 10am–9pm
Jiyugaoka station, South exit

Jiyugaoka is a precinct made for bookstores, like this messy little retro one that's perfect for an afternoon browse or a lengthy rifle. There's not much room at Tokyo Shobo – it's basically two aisles stuffed with vintage novels and English and Japanese art and picture books – but it's perfect if your idea of fun is sifting through teetering mountains of old magazines and second-hand books. You'll find kids' books here too, including stories about that adorable rabbit Miffy, which look even better written in kanji. One of the really fun things about the store are the 1980s editions of cult Japanese magazine *Popeye*, with its over-the-top hairstyles, make-up and pop fashions.

3

CHECK & STRIPE

2-24-13 Midorigaoka,
Meguro-ku
6421 3200
www.checkandstripe.com
Open Mon–Sun 10am–7pm
Jiyugaoka station, South exit

Fashion designers, crafters and hobbyists are in for a treat at Check & Stripe, which stocks high-quality yet affordable fabrics. As you'd expect, it has its fair share of checked and striped material, but there's a whole range of other patterns available too, including floral and Liberty designs. The fabrics for sale are simple and modern, very Japanese but with a knowing nod to French and English aesthetics. Expect fine-spun cottons and textural linens. Complement your textile purchases with items from the extensive range of buttons, ribbons, trims and decals. If you need added inspiration, the store has its own range of craft books – the text is Japanese only, but where there's a will there's a way ... Its Kichijoji store is more of the same: cute outside and in, and ready to set you up for that burst of creativity.

4

D&DEPARTMENT

8-3-2 Okusawa, Setagaya-ku
5752 0120
Open Mon–Sun 12–8pm (shop);
Thurs–Tues 11.30am–11pm
(cafe)
Jiyugaoka station, South exit,
or Kuhonbutsu station

A short walk from Kuhonbutsu station, or a lovely stroll from Jiyugaoka, this flagship D&Department store is part cafe, part design shop and part vintage retail set in a converted '60s modernist warehouse. The store prides itself on showcasing the best in everyday objects by small makers and growers from all over Japan. Expect repurposed furniture and up-cycled clothing alongside soy-milk bottles, bags of rice and soybean crackers with packaging so exquisite you won't want to open it. The cafe is charming with low tables and plush armchairs from which you can enjoy a delicious curry or something from the seasonal menu. Coffee is made from beans roasted on site and goes perfectly with the maple chiffon cake. D&Department also publishes a top-notch travel magazine, which you can browse through while kicking back with a craft beer.

CHECK & STRIPE

5.

BAISHINKA TEA HOUSE

3-4-7 Yakumo, Meguro-ku
5731 1620
Open Mon–Sun 9am–5pm
Jiyugaoka station, Central exit

A lovely stroll just 15 minutes from Jiyugaoka station, this beautiful tearoom is one person's quest to bring the Zen-like beauty of the Japanese tea ceremony into the 21st century. Baishinka means 'heart of the plum' and the stunningly renovated old house is appropriately set within a garden of plum trees. The decor is traditional dark wood and antiques, updated by the clean lines of brushed concrete and glass. Head into the tearoom and ask for wagashi. The staff will present you with a beautiful wooden box of traditional seasonal sweets. Tea can be blended to taste, and the staff let you take in the aroma like it's a fine wine before pouring it for you. Sublime cutlery, ceramics and teapots add a touch of handmade elegance. Make sure to buy some exquisitely packaged presents on the way out from the gift shop.

TOKYO TIP
Nakameguro, Daikanyama
and Jiyugaoka are all
on the Tokyu–Toyoko
line, making it easy to
plan a daytrip to all
three precincts.

JIYUGAOKA BURGER

4F, 1-3-15 Jiyugaoka, Meguro-ku
6459 5133
Open Mon–Sun 11am–11pm
Jiyugaoka station, South exit

This rooftop terrace four floors up is perfect for a breeze, a burger and a craft beer on a lazy afternoon or evening. It's popular and small – there isn't even enough room to wait – so if it's too busy the staff will take your phone number and give you a buzz when there's space. Choose from classic beef or chicken burgers with various artery-hardening toppings and sauces. More adventurous options include the liver-paste burger, which was sold out when we were there, so you might want to get in early if this takes your fancy. You can even build your own burger by choosing your ingredients, but without much English on the menu you could be in for a surprise.

The burgers look insurmountable, stacked high and held together with a metal skewer. Just remember: squish down, pull the pin, get stuck in. Napkins are definitely your best friend here. There's no veggie burger on the menu, but the cheesy salsa potatoes are a sizzling pan of deliciousness, the best ¥560 a vegetarian will ever spend. Add a salad and you'll be in heaven. If you're not in intensive care by the end of your meal, order the ice-cream burger for dessert!

RA.A.G.F

5F, 1-26-3 Jiyugaoka, Meguro-ku
3725 2240
Open Mon–Sun 12–8pm
Jiyugaoka station, South exit

Bless your cotton socks Tokyo: you have more cute per square mile than any other city in the world. And Ra.a.g.f is up there with the cutest of the cute. Pop into this rabbit cafe and you'll think all your Easters have come at once. The curious name stands for the equally curious Rabbit and Grow Fat (if you were wondering), and the picture on the business card is of a cute bunny and a pile of droppings, so fair warning: watch where you step. The rabbits are in cages, but you can get your mitts on their super-soft fur by reaching in and stroking them. You can also set one or two inmates free to hop happily about the cafe. (We opted for a massive black fluff-ball called 'Figaro'.) It only costs around ¥700 for half an hour with the bunnies plus a drink – a bargain for so much adorableness – so hop in and have a thumping good time.

GETTING TO AND FROM NARITA INTERNATIONAL AIRPORT

The airport is 71 kilometres from the city. Following are some options for getting to and from Narita:

Narita Express Train

It's express, it's convenient and it's comfy. Around ¥3000 will get you a one-way ticket to Tokyo station in 53 minutes. Some trains go further to Shibuya and Shinjuku. Trains depart every 30 to 60 minutes from 7.30am to 9.45pm. There are snacks, booze and toilets onboard the trains.

Keisei Skyliner Train

For around ¥2500, the Skyliner will take you to Nippori or Ueno station, handy if you are staying near these areas, or near Asakusa. You can transfer to the Yamanote Line (*see* opposite page) at Nippori/Ueno; this can get you to Tokyo station in 10 minutes. The Skyliner runs from 8.17am to 10.30pm.

Keisei Limited Express Train

A cheaper option. Around ¥1100 will get you to Ueno, but it will take 71 minutes. If you are on a budget, and patient, this could be a good option. It operates from 5.41am to 10.30pm.

Limousine Bus

Departs every 15 to 20 minutes between 8.45am and 6.50pm and takes around 80 to 100 minutes to get to Tokyo station. It's comfy and you get to see a bit of the city on the way in. The cost is around ¥3100. Some limousine buses target specific hotels and areas, so ask for details at the airport counter. There can be delays, depending on traffic conditions.

Taxi

A very expensive option. It will cost you around ¥22,000 and take about 60 to 80 minutes, depending on the traffic.

BICYCLES

Riding a bike is a great way to get around a single precinct. You can hire bikes at many places, including Muji in Yurakucho (*see* p. 091), Tokyo Bike in Yanaka, Geographica in Meguro (*see* p. 208) and Yoyogi Park (*see* p. 028). You can even hire electric bikes! Check out http://rentabike.jp for more info.

GETTING AROUND TOWN

Police boxes are located on every few blocks and are good places for asking directions.

Trains

Grab a **Suica** or **Pasmo** card from machines at train stations. For a deposit of around ¥500, these cards are rechargeable and easy to use. Top them up at the machines (they have English instructions) and swipe them at the barrier gates to get into a station. You can also use them on buses, in station lockers, and in an increasing number of vending machines, restaurants and convenience stores.

The **Tokyo Metro** and **JR Lines** are the main train lines, but there are also privately run lines. Suica and Pasmo cards allow you to travel on all of the different lines.

BUSES

Buses within Tokyo's 23 wards are to be entered from the front. Prices are fixed (usually ¥200), so put your money into the box next to the driver, get a ticket and exit from the rear. If you have a Suica or Pasmo card, it's easiest to swipe it on entry at the front of the bus, then leave at the back.

TRAIN TIPS

Know your station exit! It is easy to get lost.

Trains run from around 5am to midnight.

Trains have women-only cars at certain times, and some seats are reserved for the elderly, injured or pregnant. If you are pregnant, you can get a 'maternity badge' at train stations to make other travellers aware and mindful of your condition.

Line up for the trains in designated areas and wait for all other passengers to get off before boarding.

Cram yourself in at peak times; it's one of the few times Tokyoites get up close and very personal.

If you have a train ticket but you're not sure whether it has enough value on it for your journey, you can adjust your fare at a fare-adjustment machine when you get to your destination.

The Yamanote Line is a circular line that stops at some of the major stations in Tokyo, and also a few surprising ones (Takadanobaba is the home of Astro Boy, and, as such, plays the Astro Boy theme as its station music). In winter the trains are warm, in summer, cool. Make a day of it! Ride the Yamanote and get off at random stations; you'll find all kinds of cool things.

Trains are great fun, comfortable and often have little TVs playing very cute advertisements to help you pass the time.

WALKING

You'll do a lot of walking in Tokyo – it's how you'll stumble across some of your best finds – so wear a good pair of shoes! At major crossings, when the pedestrian light turns green, all traffic stops and people go in all directions! It's called 'the scramble' and Shibuya's crossing is the big one. Join in the fun: when the lights change, launch yourself into the chaos. It's estimated that about 2500 people cross at Shibuya at any one time!

A map is your friend in Tokyo. Once you've found the right train station exit, look on your map for identifiable places like convenience stores, museums or banks and get your bearings from there. You can also ask at police boxes, or ask a local: they may not speak English but if you have a map, it's likely they'll walk you to your destination no matter how far out of their way they have to go.

TAXIS

Taxis are an expensive way to get around Tokyo; they cost ¥700 for the first 2 kilometres, then ¥200 for every kilometre after that. Late at night, fares can rise by 20%. All tolls will be calculated in the cost of your fare.

TAXI TIPS

Lights on the dashboard of a taxi indicate its status: red means the taxi is free, yellow means it is occupied and green means there is a night-time surcharge.

Taxi doors open and close on their own!

Ask your hotel clerk or concierge to tell taxi drivers where you are going.

Take your hotel business card with you when going out and give it to taxi drivers when you want to get back to your hotel.

HANEDA AIRPORT

Less than 30 minutes from Tokyo. Transport options include monorail, Keikyu railway, limousine buses and taxis.

BULLET TRAINS (SHINKANSEN)

Depart from Tokyo, Shinagawa and some of the other larger train stations. Buy tickets from a JR counter, a machine or use your Japan Rail Pass.

ELECTRONICS

Tokyo has great electronic gadgets and devices, but remember that they are a different wattage and the power plugs use different outlets. If you really have to buy something, you'll need to get it converted or buy a transformer device. Some stores will sell Western versions, which have already been changed over. Duty-free places at the airport will have Western-style wattage.

PHONES & WI-FI

To access wi-fi in Tokyo you have a few options. Free wi-fi is rare. Many travellers rent pocket wi-fi at Narita to use with their smart phone. You can hire a mobile phone at the airport or buy a SIM card for your phone there or at outlets around the city such as SoftBank or Docomo, Tokyo's major mobile phone providers.

An easier, and often cheaper, option is to check with your phone provider before leaving home; they often offer daily fixed prices for data downloads. Whatever you do, don't have data roaming switched on without getting a deal first — it can cost a fortune.

To call somewhere outside of Tokyo, dial 010, then the country code of where you're calling, and then the area code, dropping the initial '0'.

Tokyo's area code is 03, but you don't need to dial it if you're calling within Tokyo.

SHOPPING

When you enter a shop (or restaurant), staff will say 'irrashaimase', which means, you are welcome. There's not really an answer to this, but sometimes it's so emphatic you'll feel like saying something in return! Just say 'konnichiwa' (hello).

SHOPPING TIPS

Carry your passport with you so that if you purchase something worth over ¥10,000 in major department stores or stores that have a tax-free sign, it can be bought duty free.

Do not haggle in Tokyo, unless you are at an open-air market.

Post Office

Public Transport Maternity Badge

Seven Bank ATM

Tax Free

Free Wi-Fi

Police Box

Pronunciation is simply this: vowels are 'a' (pronounced like the 'u' in up), 'i' (pronounced like the 'i' in imp), 'u' (pronounced as the 'oo' in book), 'e' (pronounced as the 'e' in egg) and 'o' (pronounced as the 'o' in lock). This doesn't change for any word, and if two vowels are placed together, you say them as if they were separate vowel sounds in a row. Simple! The letter 'r' is pronounced as a cross between an 'r' and an 'l'; the easiest way to make this sound is to touch the roof of your mouth with the tip of your tongue.

Useful Kanji
Tokyo: 東京
Japan: 日本
Yen: 円
Male: 男
Female: 女
Enter: 入口
Exit: 出口
North: 北
South: 南
East: 東
West: 西
Try and memorise the kanji for Tokyo; it's especially useful for reading the weather on television. Male and female kanji is also useful for toilet signage in some restaurants and cafes.

Do you speak English?: anata wa eigo o hanashimasu ka?
I don't understand: wakarimasen
I don't understand Japanese: Nihongo ga wakarimasen
Hello: konnichiwa
Good morning: ohayou gozaimasu
Goodnight: oyasuminasai
Goodbye: sayonara

See you later: mata ne
Nice to meet you: hajimemashite
Please: kudasai/ onegaishimasu
Thank you: arigato, arigato gozaimasu
Thank you very much: domo arigato
Excuse me: sumimasen
How are you?: genki desu ka?
I'm well: genki desu or genki
How much is this?: ikura desu ka?
I'll take this: kore kudasai
Cheers!: kanpai!
I would like a beer please: beru wo kudasai (or add nama before beru for a draught beer)
Delicious: oishii
Can I have the bill please?: okanjo onegaishimasu?
After eating a delicious meal say: gochisousama deshita
Train station: eki
Airport: kuukou
Taxi: takushi
I love Japan!: Watashi wa Nihon ga daisuki!

EATING AND DRINKING TIPS

Most cafes and bars shut for one day during the week, so make sure you check opening hours before going out.

Many cafes open around 11am or 12pm, so keep this in mind if you need an early morning coffee fix.

It can be good fun to try the omakase, or chef's choice, at restaurants. This allows chefs to decide what they think is the best choice for you.

Ask your hotel to make restaurant reservations on your behalf if you don't speak Japanese.

Chopstick etiquette: When using chopsticks, don't stick them upright in a bowl of rice – this is a funeral custom. Also, don't pass food to or take food from other people using chopsticks, and don't spear food with these eating utensils (okay, we may have done this a few times …). Lastly, don't move a bowl towards you with chopsticks.

Regarding drinks, *do* pour other people's drinks as much as possible.

Many small eateries have plastic food models out the front of their establishment. You can take a staff member outside, point to your preferred dish and say either 'onegaishimasu' (polite) or 'kudasai' two Japanese words for 'please'.

Many cafes have pictorial menus, which is very handy if you don't speak Japanese. As above, point to your preferred dish and say either 'onegaishimasu' or 'kudasai'.

Smoking is still allowed in a lot of restaurants.

If you want to eat with salarymen and locals head to the many inexpensive and great eating options around or inside train stations.

EATING & DRINKING

Most menus in Tokyo are written in Japanese. In this book, we've noted in individual reviews where an English menu is available. We've also broken listings down in the following way: places listed under an Eat heading don't sell alcohol, but often serve tea and coffee. Those listed under Eat and Drink serve food, tea and coffee (usually) and booze.

CONVENIENCE STORES

Tokyo's convenience stores, or konbinis, are awesome. You might be used to convenience stores having higher prices for junky products, but in Tokyo they are fast, cheap, convenient and sell great stuff, including cheap beer, fresh fruit and vegetables, sweets, magazines and delicious takeaway food. Sometimes they have their own select ranges, and FamilyMarts stock Muji products. You can even buy concert and museum tickets. We could happily do a convenience-store tour of Tokyo. Sunkus, FamilyMart, Lawson, AM/PM and 7-Eleven are the main stores, but look out for cute neighbourhood versions too.

VENDING MACHINES

Vending machines are everywhere. The variety of drinks they have is staggering – convenient if you want a hot green tea or coffee in winter or cold drink at any time of the year. They can also sell anything from hamburgers to toilet paper, stationery, shirts, alcohol and cup noodles.

MANNERS

Manners are very important in Japan, so always be as polite as possible. Invoke your inner sense of calm and treat everyone with respect, and respect will be returned to you. The deeper someone bows, the more respect they are showing you. Most younger people don't bow as much now, but a slight bow of the head is always a good thing.

Take off your shoes before getting onto a tatami mat or entering a house. A lot of restaurants will also require you to remove your shoes, but the staff will let you know. There are usually slippers provided, but these are for going to the bathroom (you don't have to worry about this in more contemporary restaurants). You should even take your shoes off when entering a clothing-store changing room.

If you're sick with a cold, buy a face mask. Also, don't take a wet umbrella into a shop; use the bags or holders provided. (Note: grab a clear plastic umbrella from konbinis or stands at the train stations if it's raining; they are cheap and well made.)

Crime is low in Tokyo. There are very few dangerous areas. Honestly, you could drop your wallet and someone will pick it up and give it back to you, or if you left it somewhere, it would likely be mailed to you.

ADDRESSES

Even Tokyoites have trouble with the city's address system — they use maps as well! Always consult a map, and navigate using nearby landmarks, shrines or convenience stores.

A typical Tokyo addresss will read like this: 5-35-1 Daita Setagaya. In order, the numbers stand for subsection (ward), block number and then building number. In Tokyo, the ground floor is referred to as the first floor (1F; the next floor up is 2F), and the floor beneath that is the basement. There's no point looking for street names as most streets don't have names! The ones that do were mostly named by the Americans after World War II to help them get around.

Please do not talk on your mobile on trains or while walking. Eating and walking is also a no-no.

TOILETS

Public toilets are easy to find and range from the basic to the so-intricate that you'll never have time to work out all of the functions. Some toilets play music, so pick a tune! The nicest toilets are located in department stores. Some public toilets are non-Western (squat) ones, so beware, or dare!

Groping on a crowded train is unapproved behaviour.

Steve Wide and Michelle Mackintosh

Michelle and Steve travel to Tokyo whenever they can. They love the food, the people, the vibrancy and the way the city is constantly evolving and yet keeps its traditional heart. They use their passion for amateur photography to document Tokyo's genius and madness, and their magpie skills to gather up little recollections and keepsakes.

Steve hosts the long-running radio show 'Far and Wide' on Melbourne's Triple R FM on which he has interviewed hundreds of UK bands. As a club DJ he has toured with many bands and performed at live festivals, and has run many of Melbourne's most enduring indie and retro club nights. He went back to university to complete his writing and editing diploma and went on to gain a Masters in creative media and writing.

Michelle is a book designer and illustrator who has won numerous design awards. She has designed dozens of books on a wide range of cultural topics from craft books to cookbooks, gardening books and city guides. She also has several ranges of stationery and is a collector of 'cute' and a self-confessed stationery nerd.

Michelle and Steve have written and illustrated six children's books. Two were picked up as primary-school textbooks, two were finalists in the Australian Publishing Awards, and all were in the Premiers' Reading Challenge. They live in Melbourne with their giant British shorthair cat Bronte.

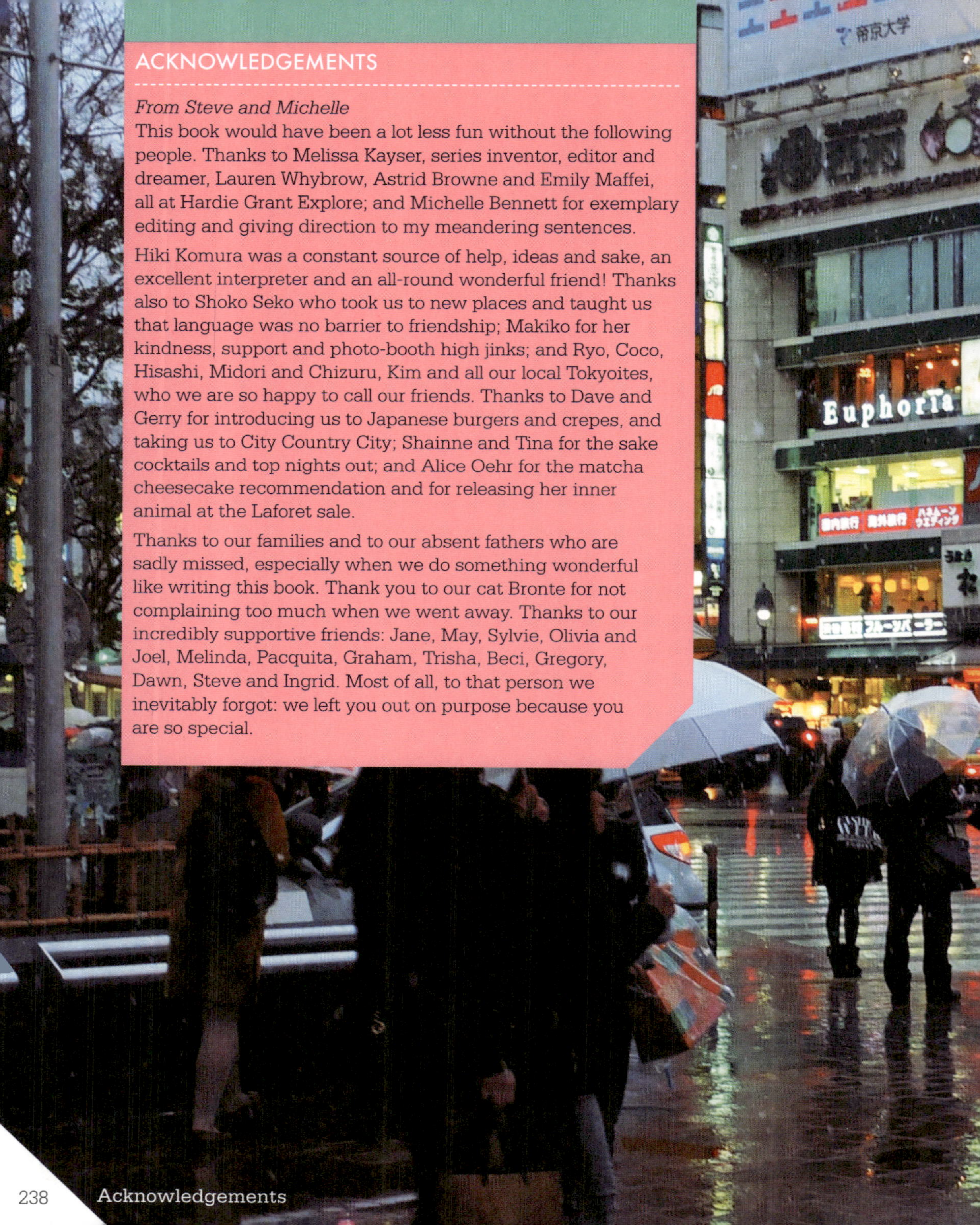

ACKNOWLEDGEMENTS

From Steve and Michelle

This book would have been a lot less fun without the following people. Thanks to Melissa Kayser, series inventor, editor and dreamer, Lauren Whybrow, Astrid Browne and Emily Maffei, all at Hardie Grant Explore; and Michelle Bennett for exemplary editing and giving direction to my meandering sentences.

Hiki Komura was a constant source of help, ideas and sake, an excellent interpreter and an all-round wonderful friend! Thanks also to Shoko Seko who took us to new places and taught us that language was no barrier to friendship; Makiko for her kindness, support and photo-booth high jinks; and Ryo, Coco, Hisashi, Midori and Chizuru, Kim and all our local Tokyoites, who we are so happy to call our friends. Thanks to Dave and Gerry for introducing us to Japanese burgers and crepes, and taking us to City Country City; Shainne and Tina for the sake cocktails and top nights out; and Alice Oehr for the matcha cheesecake recommendation and for releasing her inner animal at the Laforet sale.

Thanks to our families and to our absent fathers who are sadly missed, especially when we do something wonderful like writing this book. Thank you to our cat Bronte for not complaining too much when we went away. Thanks to our incredibly supportive friends: Jane, May, Sylvie, Olivia and Joel, Melinda, Pacquita, Graham, Trisha, Beci, Gregory, Dawn, Steve and Ingrid. Most of all, to that person we inevitably forgot: we left you out on purpose because you are so special.

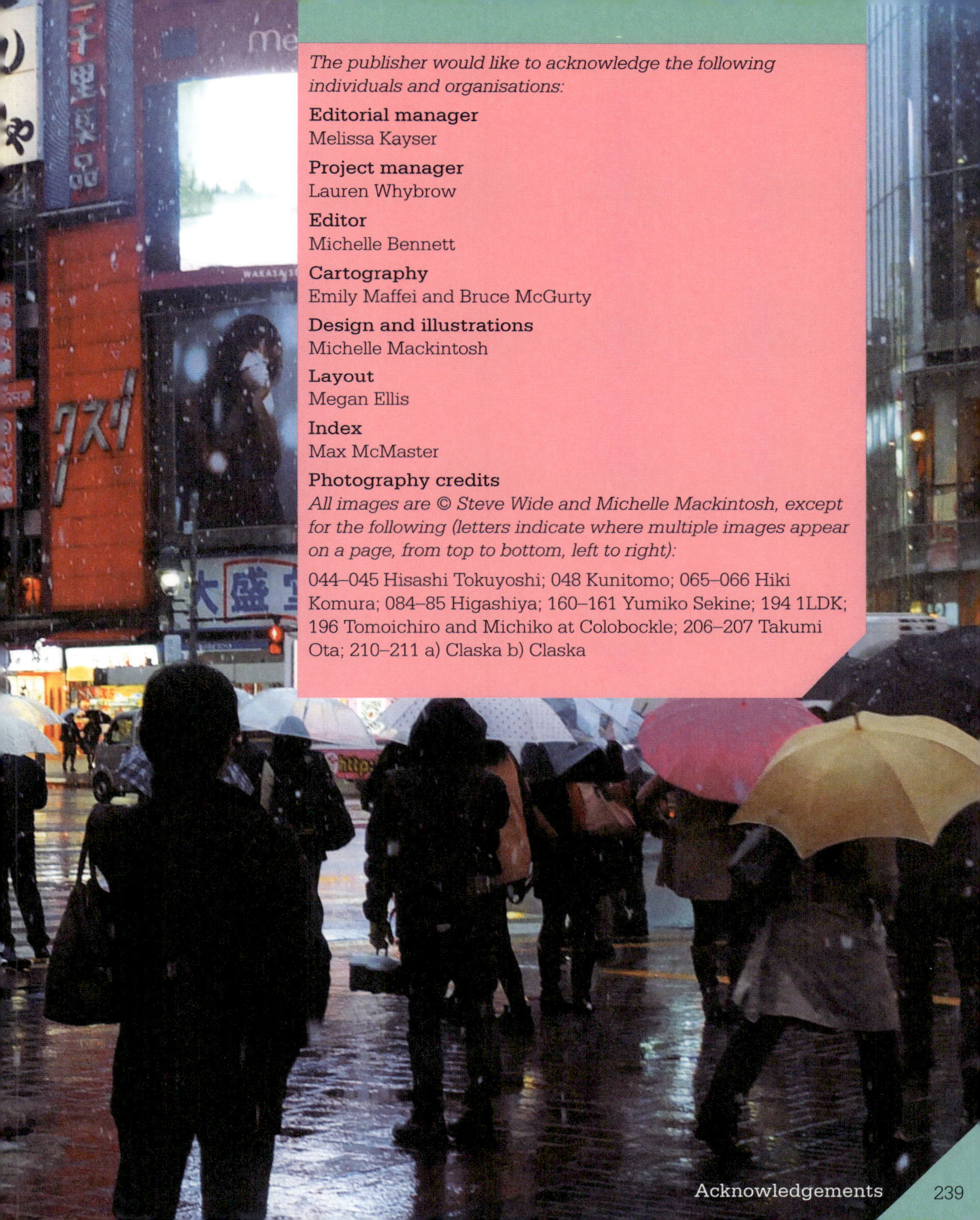

The publisher would like to acknowledge the following individuals and organisations:

Editorial manager
Melissa Kayser

Project manager
Lauren Whybrow

Editor
Michelle Bennett

Cartography
Emily Maffei and Bruce McGurty

Design and illustrations
Michelle Mackintosh

Layout
Megan Ellis

Index
Max McMaster

Photography credits
All images are © Steve Wide and Michelle Mackintosh, except for the following (letters indicate where multiple images appear on a page, from top to bottom, left to right):

044–045 Hisashi Tokuyoshi; 048 Kunitomo; 065–066 Hiki Komura; 084–85 Higashiya; 160–161 Yumiko Sekine; 194 1LDK; 196 Tomoichiro and Michiko at Colobockle; 206–207 Takumi Ota; 210–211 a) Claska b) Claska

Explore Australia Publishing Pty Ltd
Ground Floor, Building 1, 658 Church Street,
Richmond, VIC 3121, Australia

Explore Australia Publishing Pty Ltd is a division of Hardie Grant Publishing Pty Ltd

Published by Explore Australia Publishing Pty Ltd, 2015

Concept, maps, form and design © Explore Australia Publishing Pty Ltd, 2015
Text © Steve Wide and Michelle Mackintosh, 2015

A Cataloguing-in-Publication entry is available from the catalogue of the National
Library of Australia at www.nla.gov.au

The maps in this publication incorporate data © OpenStreetMap contributors.
OpenStreetMap is made available under the Open Database License: http://
opendatacommons.org/licenses/odbl/1.0/.
Any rights in individual contents of the database are licensed under the Database
Contents License: http://opendatacommons.org/licenses/dbcl/1.0/
See more at: http://opendatacommons.org/licenses/odbl/

Disclaimer

ISBN-13 9781741174687

10 9 8 7 6 5 4 3 2 1

Printed and bound in China by 1010 Printing International Ltd

Publisher's note: Every effort has been made to ensure that the information in this
book is accurate at the time of going to press. The publisher welcomes information
and suggestions for correction or improvement. Email: info@exploreaustralia.net.au

Publisher's disclaimer: The publisher cannot accept responsibility for any errors or
omissions. The representation on the maps of any road or track is not necessarily
evidence of public right of way. The publisher cannot be held responsible for any
injury, loss or damage incurred during travel. It is vital to research any proposed
trip thoroughly and seek the advice of relevant government bodies and travel
organisations before you leave.

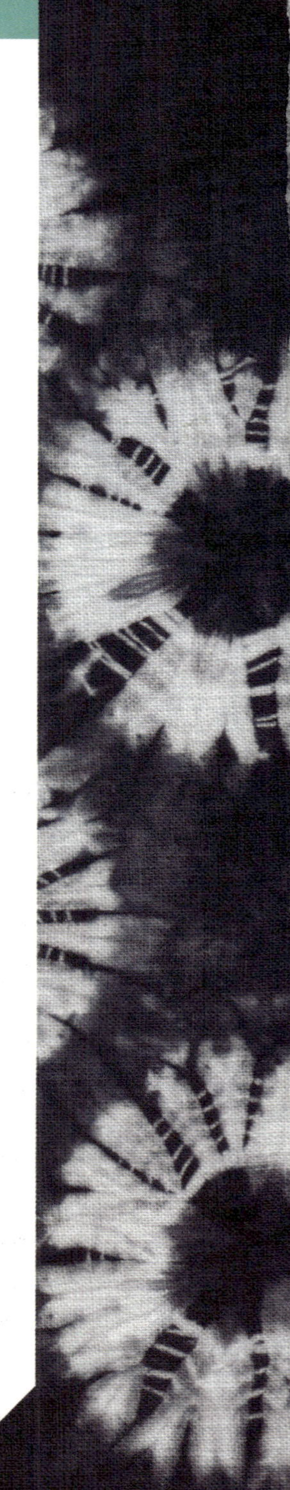